The Ins and Outs of Mesopotamia

Also from Westphalia Press
westphaliapress.org

The Idea of the Digital University

Criminology Confronts Cultural Change

Eight Decades in Syria

Avant-Garde Politician

Socrates: An Oration

Strategies for Online Education

Conflicts in Health Policy

Material History and Ritual Objects

Jiu-Jitsu Combat Tricks

Opportunity and Horatio Alger

Careers in the Face of Challenge

Bookplates of the Kings

Collecting American Presidential Autographs

Misunderstood Children

Original Cables from the Pearl Harbor Attack

Social Satire and the Modern Novel

The Amenities of Book Collecting

Trademark Power

A Definitive Commentary on Bookplates

James Martineau and Rebuilding Theology

Royalty in All Ages

The Middle East: New Order or Disorder?

The Man Who Killed President Garfield

Chinese Nights Entertainments: Stories from Old China

Understanding Art

Homeopathy

The Signpost of Learning

Collecting Old Books

The Boy Chums Cruising in Florida Waters

The Thomas Starr King Dispute

Salt Water Game Fishing

Lariats and Lassos

Mr. Garfield of Ohio

The Wisdom of Thomas Starr King

The French Foreign Legion

War in Syria

Naturism Comes to the United States

Water Resources: Iniatives and Agendas

Designing, Adapting, Strategizing in Online Education

Feeding the Global South

The Design of Life: Development from a Human Perspective

The Ins and Outs of Mesopotamia
All Rights Reserved © 2016 by Policy Studies Organization

Westphalia Press
An imprint of Policy Studies Organization
1527 New Hampshire Ave., NW
Washington, D.C. 20036
info@ipsonet.org

ISBN-13: 978-1-63391-365-3
ISBN-10: 1-63391-365-1

Cover design by Jeffrey Barnes:
jbarnesbook.design

Daniel Gutierrez-Sandoval, Executive Director
PSO and Westphalia Press

Updated material and comments on this edition
can be found at the Westphalia Press website:
www.westphaliapress.org

The Ins and Outs of Mesopotamia

by Thomas Lyell

Introduced by Paul Rich

WESTPHALIA PRESS
An Imprint of Policy Studies Organization

INTRODUCTION
by Paul Rich

It is always possible . . . to fix on certain parts of the world which are not under our control, which are not likely to be under our control, and in which events may not altogether be going according to our minds – Sir Edward Grey, in the House of Commons, 8 March 1911.

The Ins and Outs of Mesopotamia appeared in 1923 when the London house of A. M. Philpot was persuaded to publish a highly opinionated manuscript by a young British officer. Thomas Lyell was an enthusiastic participant in the occupation of Iraq that followed in the aftermath of the British invasion during the First World War. Outrageously prejudiced and bigoted, he was also intensely pragmatic and displayed a practicality reminiscent of a Benthamite (complete to the extent of an inordinate interest in the effects of nutritious vegetables). Lyell was utterly convinced of the civilizing value of a Western presence in the Middle East and believed that his book would enlighten the British public, confused as they were by the racial and religious differences that compli-

INTRODUCTION

cated and frustrated Imperial policy in Iraq. Perhaps his experiences as a magistrate for the criminal court that the British established in Baghdad contributed to his own dour view of Iraqi life. Additional service as a Tapu judge, or land claims officer, did nothing to moderate his opinions about Middle Eastern duplicity. As he makes clear, he was one of the young men who viewed Sir Arnold Wilson, sometime British Political Resident in the Gulf, as a mentor.

His was not a book written with the usual illusions about the West coming to the aid of the Arabs. Certainly Lyell did not see the situation through rose-coloured glasses when he observed: 'That the Arabs of Mesopotamia "don't want us" is nothing new. They have never wanted anyone or any form of government which could restrain their inherited instinct for lawlessness and violent crime' (page 157). He was swimming upstream, for many of his more buoyant contemporaries thought that the toppling of the Ottomans and 'freeing' of Iraq was an unreserved victory for decency which the Arabs would reciprocate by embracing democracy and order.

In my judgement no other book to emerge from the British invasion of Iraq and the subsequent civil war of 1920 gives such an insight into the mind-set of the junior British officers who were charged with the day-to-day civil administration of the conquered Arab territories. The vast majority of the accounts to come out of the period are folksy recollections of casual encounters with bedouin, Edwardian tales of camping trips and anecdotes

INTRODUCTION

about minarets and veiled women. Lyell is remarkably free of such colourful personal musings. He meets but makes no comment about St John Philby, a maverick young fellow officer who would resign his commission to become the confidant and adviser to Saudi monarchs – and spend part of the Second World War interned as a suspect Nazi sympathizer. Others of similar interest are passed by without remark, for this atrabilious book is not an anecdotal collection of reminiscences. Instead of the autobiographical journal so common in his time, Lyell produced an unusual treatise on Iraq's political prospects, with an emphasis on how Muslim religious influence affected everything and everyone. In doing this, notwithstanding his deprecation of the Arabs and of Islam, he succeeded in creating a commentary with a significance which has withstood time.

The questions he put about whether or not to leave the Iraqis to their own devices or to intervene on a large scale are similar to questions that would repeatedly be asked in ensuing decades in the corridors of Whitehall and the American State Department. His fears about the consequences of temporizing have an appropriateness to later developments: 'We should have no control over other portions of the country, in which must be produced a similar condition of insecurity to that which complete withdrawal would, admittedly, involve' (page 181). Lyell's book deserves to be rescued from obscurity and belongs on the reading-list of serious students of the present Near East.

INTRODUCTION

Lyell's own Mesopotamian career encapsulates many points made by me elsewhere – particularly in *The Invasions of the Gulf* (Allborough, 1991). He was, for example, the officer in charge of distributing the yearly beneficence of the Oudh bequest, interest from an Indian endowment which was paid to Muslim needy – an example of the Indian connections with the Middle East which have not been emphasized nearly enough.

The years have not rendered his comments less valuable or less provocative. His descriptions of Shia ceremonies could be a description of those that I have seen. His memoir is among the few we have by those who saw the legal side of the British occupation and this gave him an unusual comparative insight into Islamic customs.

Lyell was so outrageously candid that a first reaction on reading the book is that one is encountering a rabid racist polemicist. Yet he is quite fair when it comes to distributing his brickbats equally – British, Arabs, Jews, Kurds, and everyone else get their share of scorn – and, in actual fact, he could be quite measured and perspicacious: 'Many Arabs, especially among the children, have a truer knowledge of real religion than hundreds of pious Anglo-Saxons who attend their Sunday service and peruse the *Church Times* on Friday mornings' (page 59). His insistence that anyone wishing to come to terms with the Middle East must begin with Islam, and with its great festivals such as Muharram and Ramadhan, has not lost its relevance. The long discussion of Islam in Iraq which occupies the first section of the work is completely

INTRODUCTION

warranted. That is indeed the starting-point for understanding.

Despite the virulence of his criticisms of the Arabs, he is quick to defend from the charge of hypocrisy the common people who follow Islam: 'It is frequently stated by Europeans who have spent some time in the East that the fast is, comparatively speaking, mere parade, because the people are permitted to eat as they like during the night. Such a prejudiced and ignorant charge could not be made by anyone who took the least trouble to try to understand and sympathise with the people among whom he lives . . .' (page 64). His discussion of Muslim marriage customs is much less prejudiced and one-sided than many more recent descriptions.

Lyell's forays into anthropological speculation about the progress of the peoples of the world deserve little respect, but possibly a dose of his pessimism (or *realpolitik*) is what is needed to redress recent American expectations of the New World Order in the Gulf.

Readers faced with Lyell's grim estimation of the post-war situation will begin to feel a sense of *déjà vu*. They will find that is an experience recurring in the ensuing pages, especially when they encounter his argument for increased intervention: 'I do not enter into the question of the Armenian and other Christian minorities; but no conceivable guarantees in the world would ensure their safety, and it is hardly possible to doubt what the European conscience would have to say. Other effects on the social life of the people as a whole would clearly follow, with consequences one could only estimate with dismay. All modern civilisation and progress would be wiped out' (page 179). This sounds plausible in the light of the continuing litany of woe through years of minority troubles, climaxing in the 1990s with the televised deaths of Kurds, Shias and (let it be emphasized) Sunnis from military action and from hunger, fatigue and cold. What is debatable is whether those who were 'saved' in the war of 1991 will in 2001 feel any better than those who were 'freed' in 1920 felt in ensuing decades.

British heroes, American victors, Arab stand-ins

The history of the British conquest of Iraq and of the subsequent bungled attempts to administer the country is largely British-written. Will a Kuwaiti or an Iraqi write the definitive book about events in the contemporary Gulf? The heroes of Arabia so far, rather embarrassingly, are invariably Westerners. When naming great figures of the region, even the well read would think first of Lawrence or, now, Stormin' Norman. Nobody remembers Muslim figures from the First World War or from the Iraq–Kuwait war – unless they remember losers such as the Ottoman Caliph or Saddam Hussain. Lawrence, incidentally, does not get preferential treatment from Lyell, who quite correctly points out that it was the hard cash that was being distributed that accounted for much of the Arab enthusiasm for the enigmatic colonel (page 161).

INTRODUCTION

The heroes are Westerners because the historians of Arabia are Westerners. Asked to list historians of Arabia, the erudite will think of Palfrey, Blunt and Burton, or more recently of Philby, Wilson and Lorimer. The exploits or outrages of expatriates in the Arab lands are chronicled by expatriates. The inhabitants are spectators, and do not even get good seats at the show. The Iraqi destruction in 1990–91 of the Kuwait archives, libraries and museums only seemed to confirm dire suspicions among some Western academics that the Arabs were not capable of preserving their heritage, let alone writing about it or understanding it. Such virulent racist pessimism would have found a favourable response from Lyell, who wrote about Iraq: 'I believe that it is possible to produce a self-governing Mesopotamia (in the *real* sense) in say one hundred years' time; but I am also convinced that it is hardly likely to be done in less . . .' (page 183).

The full story of incursions during the First World War into what is now Iraq went without much remark both during the 1990–91 hostilities and while, in the aftermath, American and British troops set up enclaves to protect the Iraqis against themselves. Perhaps this is not surprising, for the matter of the earlier invasion and subsequent occupation has been treated in the past by Middle East authorities in academia as an isolated phenomenon, one not related to evolving Imperial policy in the Gulf in the years that led up to the conflict.[1] The fact remains, however, that neither the chaos of our own times nor the strikingly simi-

INTRODUCTION

lar chaos of the past invasion and occupation can be understood without some knowledge of the background; this makes Lyell's volume of tremendous value to us. Nobody I have ever lent it to, Arab or American or British, has failed to be enraged or enlightened by it.

Gloom and money

Lyell was not the only pessimist about the Gulf. In 1902 while Viceroy of India, Lord Curzon gloomily predicted that the Baghdad Railway scheme would 'rivet' the Kaiser's unpleasant attention on the area. The railway surely would be merely the opening gambit in a predestined succession of humiliations and assuredly would be followed by a German naval base in the Gulf; the Germans would proceed to threaten the British route to India; and the Gulf shaikhdoms would have another suitor. To forestall this domino disaster, the Government of India increased its political interest in Kuwait and sided with the Shaikh of Kuwait in his claims to Bubiyan Island, a possible terminus for the railway.[2] Restless nights in the Foreign Office were caused by contemplating that 'the whole of Mesopotamia is overrun by German commercial travellers'.[3]

As has so often been the predicament for any intervening powers in the Gulf, the British were torn between increasing their own presence and avoiding a strain on resources. While Mesopotamia or Iraq seemed ripe for the plucking, would the entanglement be worth the effort or the money? Lyell

INTRODUCTION

is preoccupied with how such a presence might pay for itself. Indeed, economics was part and parcel of policy deliberations in the entire period 1897–1914, a period which was marked by the Anglo-German Baghdad Railway negotiations, by concerns about protecting India's flank, and by an increasing interest in the strategic value of oil.

British financial interests in the area were considerable: in 1900–2 the total tonnage of ships calling at Basra was 478,000 and of that 453,000 tons were under the British flag. The river trade had been dominated by the British-owned Euphrates and Tigris Steam Navigation Company since 1859. The British consul in Baghdad, usually appointed by the Indian Political Service, was given the comfortable colonial title of 'Resident' and had the most impressive house in the city, as well as such ritualistic accoutrements as a detachment of sepoys as an 'honorary guard'. He was the father-protector of the large and growing Indian community settled in Mesopotamia.[4]

On 5 May 1903 Lord Lansdowne, former Viceroy of India, rose in the Lords to lay out what was later heralded as a Monroe Doctrine, British Empire style, for the Middle East.[5] The Gulf was British. However, to imply as some have that from that moment the ambiguity vanished about German intrusions in the region would be misleading. The process of alienation was gradual. Between 1903 and 1907 views on the German construction of a Baghdad line went through a metamorphosis, moving gradually from tacit approval of some sort of British financial support and even the provision

INTRODUCTION

of a subsidy for carrying Indian mail to a distinct coldness as the Anglo-Franco-Russian front coalesced.[6] The signals sent to the Germans were confusing, as were the American signals sent to the Iraqis before the start of *that* Gulf war.

Taking the plunge

'The British ruled Iraq from the First World War until 1932,' commented Albert Hourani, frankly stating what many prefer to skirt, and adding that a feeling of having done considerable good by this *de facto* annexation was widespread among British officials, a view shared by the most influential Arab political thinker of the era, George Antonius.[7] Now, with the deep divisions of Iraq ever more apparent in the aftermath of the American adventure, it is evident that the farraginous nation-state which was patched together by Lyell and his colleagues has never been very viable.

What was Iraq before there was an Iraq? The British plunged into the morass which is now Iraq (and what was at the time Turkish Arabia or Mesopotamia) without nearly enough appreciation of the effects of the long period when the region was divided into three separately administered provinces of the Ottoman Empire (vilayets) – Mosul, Baghdad and Basra. There were no Iraqis as such in 1918 and the territory that was forced to become Iraq was as heterogeneous an area as could be found in the horrendously heterogeneous Middle East. Any unity Mesopotamia did possess was given it by the Tigris and Euphrates, those

INTRODUCTION

rivers of long history and exotic commerce *par excellence*.

The landing of an Indian Expeditionary Force at Basra in 1914 and the subsequent military campaigns not only brought the Turkish rule to an end but introduced rule by the old-boy 'heaven born' or 'pedestal mob', the crack administrators of the Indian Political Service. Before the British finished their benighted occupation, this cadre and its successors had created an Iraqi identity of sorts. The Indian Political Service had been up to the same kind of work further down the Gulf, a subject I deal with in *The Invasions of the Gulf*. Creating ruling élites was a speciality of theirs.

As there was no sense of national identity to start with, the results were mixed; it is not surprising that Saddam Hussain has been only one of a long line of twentieth-century Iraqi politicians who have tried unsuccessfully to strengthen nationalistic feelings in the face of glaring and bitter geographic, racial, religious and cultural divisions.

Such divisions in Iraq go back many centuries. In Lyell's time Mosul looked towards Aleppo; Basra was the sometime capital of the Gulf; Baghdad's communications were Persian oriented. The embattled Kurds in the north and the Shia in the south need no introduction, but there were and are other minorities to whom the whole idea of an Iraq was a novelty and today is a burden, including Assyrians, a variety of Christian sects and Turks.

The British incursion was not a philanthropic one, as any reader of Lyell will quickly realize. The

INTRODUCTION

inhabitants of the newly created state were expected and forced to pay their share of the Ottoman debt as well as the expenses of the Iraqi army and of the British occupiers. This imposition averaged about 40 per cent of the total budget in the years of the Mandate. The total bill for the generous yearly salaries of the British administrators in the 1920s exceeded the annual total expenses of the country on all levels and kinds of education.[8]

Nor was the occupation really ended when Iraq entered the League of Nations (3 October 1932). The last British adviser to the Interior Ministry was tenaciously still serving in 1950, and the last British Chief Justice, Sir John Prichard, was retired from the bench only in 1951.[9] As for the military, 'Largely because the oilfields and the Empire air route were too important to be left unprotected, British troops did not in fact leave in 1928, or in 1932, and air bases were maintained in Iraq until 1958.'[10] Iraq for decades was 'a dormant British asset, which could be capitalized in the interest of Imperial strategy whenever need arose'.[11]

Initial constraints and restraints

Like the 1990–91 Iraq–Kuwait war, the Gulf war of 1914 started with a limited military build-up that soon escalated. Initially there was much talk about restraint. In October 1914 the 'Uncrowned King of the Gulf', the Political Resident Sir Percy Cox, fretted that the Indian troops being sent to Bahrain might provoke a war that he didn't want;

INTRODUCTION

a few weeks later, he had managed to convince himself that the taking of Baghdad was inevitable and desirable. A relentless and quite logical progression drew the British further and further into the black hole of Arab politics. The taking of Basra seemed sensible as a way to guard against any Turkish attack on Kuwait or Muhammara. Russian backing for the incursion made a large invasion more feasible, although a joker was that the threatened disintegration of the Russian Empire became a factor later – a parallel to the Kremlin's problems being everyone's problems today.[12]

From the beginning of the débâcle, a driving force behind the campaign was a pair of less than congenial partners, the India Office in London and the Government of India. While both opposed proposals that a measure of internationalization be attempted by including a small Japanese force or Chinese troops in any Mesopotamian operation,[13] generally the two bureaucracies did not see eye to eye. The Government of India in the events leading up to the war had been much more concerned about the Russians than the India Office had been, and 'The India Office was itself chiefly responsible for the exclusion of the Indian Government from the formulation of Britain's Mesopotamian policy.'[14] Not consulted in any of these machinations were the Indian soldiers who were soon to die unpleasantly in such large numbers.

What the India Office and the Government of India did agree about was that the Gulf was part of the Indian Empire, and that a show of force in Iraq was necessary to keep the Germans and the

INTRODUCTION

Turks from any adventures along its shores. Sir R. T. Ritchie (1854–1912), stolid Secretary to the Political Department of the India Office in 1901–10 and its Permanent Under-Secretary in 1910–12, wrote in 1905: 'We are to some extent committed by our actions at Kuwait and Bubiyan Island to the view that the rly [sic] from Baghdad to the sea is an Indian interest.'[15] Indeed, in December 1914 it seemed that this strategy had really worked and there was (echoes of a word much used in 1991 about a later war) 'a sense of euphoria' about the results.[16]

A point worthy of note, especially when considering the part played by air power in the Iraq–Kuwait war of 1991, is that air power was equally important in the Iraq theatre in 1914–18. There initially were sceptics, but the Royal Air Force and the enthusiasts of its newly formed Australian counterpart were so effective in bombing and frightening the Arabs and Turks that air power became a permanent part of strategy in Iraq and was a major factor in the 1920s and 1930s. This was in contrast to the single-handed style of the Indian Political Service administration of the Gulf shaikhdoms: 'Perhaps the most serious long-term consequence of the ready availability of air control was that it developed into a substitute for administration. Several incidents during the Mandate period indicate that the speed and simplicity of air attack was preferred to the more time-consuming and painstaking investigation of grievances and disputes. With such powers at its disposal the Iraq Government was not encouraged to develop less vi-

INTRODUCTION

olent methods of extending its control over the country.'[17]

Southern Iraq had been occupied by November 1914 and so Sir Percy Cox, the Political Resident for the Gulf, found himself embroiled in setting up a civil administration. The campaign during the ensuing months went according to the most optimistic plans, so smoothly in fact that by October 1915 the British were only 50 miles from Baghdad. News from the main war in Europe being disappointing, there was a buoyancy about the evident superiority of the generalship in the Middle East, and there continued the preceding autumn's 'sense of euphoria over the apparently spectacular successes'.[18] Shortly, though, disaster was to replace elation, and terrible reverses at Kut postponed the triumphant entry into Baghdad for a year.

As the troops pressed on, the large areas captured were being administered by hastily conscripted products of the Indian civil services, and in particular the Indian Political Service officers that Cox recruited. They brought with them the administrative techniques and rituals of the Indian Empire. Many had opinions similar to Lyell's. Uniformly they were devoted products of that unique institution, the English public school. Moreover, many of the more senior and important in their ranks were confirmed 'Gulfites', IPS officers who so far had made their careers in the Gulf shaikhdoms and who looked towards going back to running the shaikhdoms when the Iraq escapade came to an end.

INTRODUCTION
Stalky & Co.

As if to confirm that a schoolboy adventure was afoot, General L. C. Dunsterville appeared on the scene in 1918 to lead one of the more minor but splendid forays, an attack on the new Bolshevik menace on the Persian frontier. He was the real-life hero of Rudyard Kipling's classic public-school story *Stalky & Co.* 'Dunsterville had not achieved the career that Kipling had forecast for him,' writes Charles Carrington in his biography *Rudyard Kipling* (1955). 'By some mischance he had missed, not only the campaigns in Burma, Egypt, and South Africa in which successful generals had made their names, but also the more spectacular events in campaigns on the Indian frontier.' Kipling by his Army connections rescued Dunsterville from the obscurity of escorting behind-the-lines trainloads of soldiers in France, and via the North-West Frontier 'Stalky' found his way to the Middle East and glory. Thus the novelist was able to make his fiction come true. There was still an exotic story-book atmosphere to soldiering.

Mesopotamia, needless to add, was not India, but Percy Cox and his *alter ego*, Arnold Wilson, had dreams of a new viceregal Middle Eastern empire for the Indian Political Service to run. Much grief was to result from their ill-advised ambitions. A loyal but somewhat obsequious 'kitchen cabinet' in Basra, which included the redoubtable Gertrude Bell, did little to dissuade them in their dreams. About the only individual who comes out

INTRODUCTION

of the confusion with real credit is Sir Arthur Hirtzel:

> In fact Hirtzel at the India Office is the one authority whose attitude scarcely changed from 1914 to 1921, who recognised that Indianisation would not be possible in Mesopotamia even before the implications of President Wilson's anti-annexation pronouncements were appreciated. Throughout 1919 and 1920 he wrote to [Arnold] Wilson in Baghdad, emphasising time and time again that no form of veiled protectorate would be acceptable to the League.[19]

Arnold Wilson was deaf to warnings. He was the quintessential public-school old boy, superbly self-confident, and this great confidence caused him to apply an Indian model in the face of Hirtzel's fears.[20] Such are the ways of a bureaucracy that when the machinery is in the hands of an accomplished practitioner he is able to exercise his prejudices even when the results become a rout. That was Wilson's misfortune and to a considerable extent the source of Iraq's troubles up until now.

Wilson and Cox thought they had a solution to Iraq's difficulties and their own in monarchy, and soon were looking about for a suitable potentate, one who would join the royalty they were securing in place further south in the various shaikhdoms. To his credit, Lyell is scornful of the scheme. Simply put, monarchy was perceived as the alternative to anarchy.

INTRODUCTION

Anarchy

In 1920 stark anarchy had descended on Iraq. Former Ottoman officers, Shia religious, avaricious tribesmen and Kurdish nationalists all rose up and during the summer of 1920 there was virtually no government. Cox had to take over sole control of the British presence when a discredited Wilson resigned and went to work for an oil company. Clearly the decision on a suitable royal family could no longer be postponed. The Magib of Baghdad, Sayid Talib of Basra, the Shaikh of Muhammerah, Ibn Saud, the Aga Khan, and a Turkish prince Bourhan Ed-din were suggested.

In the meantime Winston Churchill had made a comeback after his fall from grace over the Dardanelles. Losing his Admiralty portfolio in 1915 and briefly serving with his regiment at the front, Churchill had been brought back by Lloyd George as Minister of Munitions (1917) and then to the War Office (1918–21). T. E. Lawrence (Lawrence of Arabia) was well pleased. In *Seven Pillars of Wisdom* he wrote: Mr Winston Churchill was entrusted by our harassed Cabinet with the settlement of the Middle East; and in a few weeks, at his conference in Cairo [1921], he made straight all the tangle, finding solutions fulfilling (I think) our promises in letter and spirit (where humanly possible) without sacrificing any interest of our Empire or any interest of the peoples concerned.'

Churchill in 1921–22 was Colonial Secretary and he set his mind on the young Hashemite prince Faisal;[21] given the daily bloodshed, Cox felt

INTRODUCTION

that 'an announcement of *fait accompli* would be a welcome relief to the majority of the people of Mesopotamia . . .'.[22] A referendum handily produced a resounding 96 per cent vote in favour of Faisal as king, and he was crowned in Baghdad on 23 August 1921. Like his brother rulers in the Gulf shaikhdoms, he soon needed no coaching in regal airs. The honeymoon was over by the spring of 1922, when, after being treated to a show of royal independence and truculence, Cox complained to Churchill: 'Faisal unmistakably displayed the cloven hoof. I have endeavoured to be absolutely straightforward and frank to him, and to treat him like a brother, but there you are, when he is scratched deep enough the racial weakness displays itself.'[23]

Oil on the tapis

Contrary to an uninformed but popular view that oil was not high on the British agenda during the First World War, this issue contributed considerably to the concern about the Gulf, Iraq and Iran (Persia). The prospects of large petroleum reserves that could be controlled by the British were definitely a factor in the invasion of Iraq. Stuart Cohen supports this thesis: 'As early as 1900, O'Conor [Sir N. R. O'Conor, 1843–1908; British Ambassador at Constantinople, 1898–1908] had demonstrated the relationship of the Baghdad Railway concession to the petroleum fields. By 1904 Newmarch [L. S. Newmarch, 1879–1930, Resident, Turkish Arabia, 1902–6] had verified the existence of significant deposits . . .'[24] In 1912 a British Royal Commission advised Winston Churchill as First Lord of the Admiralty that defence strategy required a secure petroleum supply. The American control of most of the world's oil was regarded with mounting anxiety. A result was that the British Government purchased 51 per cent of the Anglo-Persian Oil Company just before the start of the war in 1914 and so was directly involved in exploration and production in the region.[25]

In March 1914 the Turks announced plans to organize an oil company for Iraq. The same month, the British Foreign Office pointedly and sharply reminded Constantinople that the boundary between Iraq and Kuwait was to be strictly observed.[26] So oil definitely was part of the provocation and the motivation for the British push to Baghdad.

Events surrounding the British invasion of Iraq in 1914 have a remarkable resemblance to the events surrounding the Allied invasion in 1991. At each stage of the developing crisis, intentions were grossly misread, bureaucracies were predictably preoccupied with their own agendas rather than the overall problem, and the diplomats on the spot were ignored. Perhaps the Foreign Office was too anti-German, perhaps nobody had enough regard for Turkish feelings, and perhaps the Germans underestimated the British possessiveness towards the Gulf. In any event, by 1910 the British had reasoned themselves into a rigid policy and the

INTRODUCTION

tentative reformulation of this policy in the period 1910–14 came too late to head off catastrophe.

Though the British diplomatic shopping-list became more modest at the last moment, thoughts had begun to turn to ultimatums. The Gulf Indian Political Service officers, particularly Cox and Wilson, took a hard line. The contradictions between Kuwait's *de jure* ties with Turkey and its *de facto* ties with the Government of India became increasingly troublesome.

There was sound advice offered, had anyone wished to listen, to the effect that a limited operation would not be feasible if the British invaded. Partly because of this Winston Churchill wisely hoped that diplomacy would prevent a combination between Turkey and the Triple Alliance. As an alternative to invasion, a blockade of the Gulf was considered, thus cutting off trade to Baghdad and Basra. The War Office was leery of trying to occupy Basra. There were other options. The Turks maintained a garrison in Qatar, half-way down the Gulf, and the Government of India thought that ousting it and imposing a limited occupation of Qatar was a possibility.

Similarities suggest themselves between the British situation in Iraq with which Lyell is concerned and later situations. There was anxiety over what effect a full-scale invasion would have on worldwide Muslim opinion, and whether there would be an attack of Anglophobia. Many people died after, rather than during the war, as many died in the aftermath of the American chastisement of Saddam Hussain. It was not certain how

INTRODUCTION

many died in 1920 and similarly unknown would be the exact number who died in 1991: 'The unquiet dead have many ways of haunting – particularly in the Middle East, which has been accumulating the grievances of the dead for thousands of years.'[27]

Lyell's confidence in British abilities to straighten out the Iraqi quagmire proved unfounded. American hopes for lasting results from their 1990–91 intervention seemed equally ill fated. And further comparisons come to mind. A whole region and generation were brutalized by the Mesopotamian campaigns, not only physically but psychologically. That, too, happened again. A sign in the International Hotel in Kuwait City in April 1991 invited visitors to put their names down on the 'Interrogation and Torture Media Sign-up' if they wanted to interview bereaved families. The Kuwaitis developed a new sport, racing along the highways firing guns into the air to celebrate – what? A realization dawned that problems had intensified, not disappeared. Getting into the Gulf once more proved easier than getting out.

NOTES

1. See Stuart A. Cohen, *British Policy in Mesopotamia, 1903–1914*, Ithaca Press (published for The Middle East Centre, St Antony's College, Oxford), 1976, 1–3. I have cited three authors – Cohen, Mejcher and Sluglett – to give readers access to three well-balanced treatments of issues of the era with good bibliographies, but those familiar with them will note my disagreement with some of their views. They provide a good starting-point for those who wish to explore the subject. So does Briton Cooper Busch, *Britain, India and the Arabs, 1914–1921*, University of California Press,

INTRODUCTION

Berkeley, 1971. Also see the bibliography in my book *The Invasions of the Gulf*, Allborough Press, Cambridge, 1991.

2. Cohen, *British Policy in Mesopotamia*, 48–49.

3. Foreign Office (hereafter FO) 800/61: E. Grey (Viscount Grey of Falladon), FO Memorandum, 1 August 1907, qtd Cohen, *British Policy in Mesopotamia*, 53.

4. Cohen, *British Policy in Mesopotamia*, 8–9.

5. Helmut Mejcher, *Imperial Quest for Oil: Iraq 1910–1928*, Ithaca Press (published for The Middle East Centre, St Antony's College, Oxford), 1976, 10.

6. Cohen, *British Policy in Mesopotamia*, 31–32. It has been asserted that there was no British policy towards Mesopotamia in 1903. Ibid., 35.

7. In a preface to Peter Sluglett, *Britain in Iraq, 1914–1932*, Ithaca Press (published for The Middle East Centre, St Antony's College, Oxford), 1976, i. Sluglett made use of the Baghdad High Commission papers, which are in the National Archives of India.

8. Sluglett, *Iraq Under British Occupation*, 5, 8 n. 12.

9. Ibid., 8 n. 9.

10. Ibid., 260.

11. Mejcher, *Imperial Quest for Oil*, 174.

12. See esp. Mejcher, *Imperial Quest for Oil*, 26.

13. Ibid., 28.

14. Cohen, *British Policy in Mesopotamia*, 74.

15. India Office Library: L/P&S/10, Vol. 87, No. 1905/3131, Minute on 27 June 1905, qtd Cohen, *British Policy in Mesopotamia*, 74.

16. Sluglett, *Iraq Under British Occupation*, 10.

17. Ibid., 268–69.

18. Ibid., 12.

19. Ibid., 26.

20. See ibid., 26–27.

21. Mejcher, *Imperial Quest for Oil*, 79.

22. FO 371/6349: Telegram 148S to S/S India, 2 January 1921, qtd Sluglett, *Iraq Under British Occupation*, 46.

23. NCO730/21/21941, Cox to Shuckburgh, 28 April 1922, qtd Mejcher, *Imperial Quest for Oil*, 81.

24. Cohen, *British Policy in Mesopotamia*, 57.

25. Sluglett, *Iraq Under British Occupation*, 104–8.

26. Mejcher, *Imperial Quest for Oil*, 15–16.

27. Lance Morrow, 'A Moment for the Dead', *The Times*, 1 April 1991, 82. 'It was not, in the final analysis, deliberate deception that underlay Britain's problems in the Middle East, but the unforeseen

INTRODUCTION

and unplanned contradictions arising from unexpected pressures in a new world – and the imperfection of man.' Busch, *Britain, India and the Arabs*, 485.

THE INS AND OUTS

OF

MESOPOTAMIA

by
Thomas Lyell

LATE OF THE CIVIL ADMINISTRATION; ASSISTANT DIRECTOR OF TAPU
AND DISTRICT MAGISTRATE, BAGHDAD

1923

To

FRANCIS

THE BELOVED PHYSICIAN

IN MEMORY OF

THE MANY HAPPY YEARS WE SPENT TOGETHER IN

THE PROMISED LAND.

IN MEMORY OF

OUR LOVES AND HATES, JOYS AND SORROWS,

DIFFICULTIES AND ENCOURAGEMENTS,

AND, ABOVE ALL,

OF THAT MOST PRICELESS AND PRECIOUS GIFT OF THE GODS,

OUR FRIENDSHIP.

IN MEMORY OF ALL THESE AND MUCH BESIDES

THIS BOOK IS DEDICATED

BY

THE AUTHOR

October 1922

NAJAF, SHOWING PART OF THE GREAT WALL SURROUNDING THE CITY

The Golden Dome of the Shrine of Ali in the centre.

PREFACE

The following pages were written to put clearly before English readers the real character, beliefs, and preferences of the people of Mesopotamia, or Iraq. It includes a careful analysis of the Prophet's teaching in the Quran, especially in relation to social customs and political organisation, with an explanation of the additions to, and diversions from, the orthodox Sunnat – or Traditions – which have developed from the Shia' Imams, whom Mesopotamia accepts.

Being firmly convinced, as I am, from close personal acquaintance, that the Creed of Islam is unprogressive, personally enervating, and destructive of any instinct for citizenship, social integrity or national aspirations, I have endeavoured to show that the Muslim, and particularly the Shia', is – and for many years must remain – totally unfit for self-government, which he only 'desires' as an opportunity to escape from all law and order.

To illustrate and establish this opinion, I have described in detail the great 'Holy Cities' of Mesopotamia – scarcely known to English readers – the religious ceremonies of the people, their laws, their habits, and their characteristics, with many anecdotes from my experience of the law courts.

PREFACE

In the Second Part I have endeavoured to summarise the whole progress of events in Mesopotamia since the war; to penetrate the most complicated issues (on which the fate of our Empire depends) that have led up to our present policy; and to show how Muslim intrigue, following the psychology revealed in earlier chapters, has been at work to undermine our already diminished prestige among our Indian subjects.

If we were forced, perhaps, to compromise with Mecca (to replace the Turkish alliance), and even to talk sentiment about 'cultural autonomy', I maintain that the present weakness of our administration must lead to a disastrous collapse, with consequences that would inflame the whole world.

Above all, since the seeds of Bolshevism are spreading through all Islam, no less in Mesopotamia and India than among the Turks, it would be the height of folly for us, even partially, to evacuate these lands. I have indicated, in my final chapter upon The Future, what I believe to be the only possible line of policy: to 'steady' the East, to maintain our prestige with Islam, and, by developing Iraq's immense resources, to secure some ultimate return for British outlay and British work.

* * * *

Of Sir Arnold Wilson, our Chief from 1917–20, I might have written much. He was an unique example of what an iron determination, coupled with an apparently inexhaustible capacity for hard work and exceptional intellectual brilliancy, could accomplish. For inefficiency and flabbiness he had

PREFACE

no manner of use. Many indeed were the gifts with which he was endowed, but one stood out above all – that of inspiring each of his officers with a sense of his own personal friendship, based upon a common aim and purpose.

It is no exaggeration to say that during the dark days of 1919–20 there were not a few who cheerfully held on, bearing a strain that at times was well nigh unbearable, because they knew that their Chief was bearing it with them. Sooner than let him down, they were prepared to lose their lives – as indeed some did.

It is more than a privilege – and I use the word in no mere conventional sense – that my experience of political work and my knowledge of Mesopotamia were gathered under so great a leader and so loyal a friend.

I have to record my grateful thanks to Maulvi Muhammad Ali, of the Woking Islamic Mission, for his permission to use his translation of the Quran. I have used his version in preference to any other, as in a book of this kind a translation by a Muslim has so obvious a value.

T.L.

CONTENTS

PART I

THE FAITH AND CUSTOMS OF MESOPOTAMIA

CHAPTER I

THE HOLY CITIES OF SHIA' ISLAM 13

Life in Najaf. Story of Ali. The 'Holy' men. Orthodox Sunni, unorthodox Shia'. Training and power of the Mujtahid. The city.

CHAPTER II

SHIA' OBLIGATIONS..31

How religion rules their whole life. Stories of the prevailing avarice. The obligation, and the profits, of charity. Tyranny of the 'Holy'.

CHAPTER III

MUHARRAM 45

The obligation of penance. The martyrdom of Hussein. Head-cutting and breast-beating. The 'merit' of suffering.

CHAPTER IV

FASTING AND RAMADHAN 61

Effects on work. A *genuine* fast. Comparison with Christian 'practice'. The great feast.

CONTENTS

CHAPTER V

SHIA' AND SUNNI 75

Shia' doctrine, the Saints. Need for a 'spiritual' or supernatural (i.e. divinely appointed) leader, to preserve unity. Unique position of Ali. The people did *not* want Feisal. Narrowness and isolation of the Shia'.

CHAPTER VI

CRIME 93

Taxes by blackmail. Blood-money, and a vendetta. Complex land-tenure. The Law of Inheritance. Criminal types of three faiths. The brutal Kurd.

CHAPTER VII

CONJUGAL RELATIONSHIP AND DIVORCE 113

Teaching compared with practice. Greater laxity in 'interpreting' the Quran among the Shia'. Concubinage and the 'temporary marriage'. Demoralising to manhood. Customs and ceremonies. The dowry. *Official* restrictions to divorce largely ignored. Moral depravity of the Holy Cities. Anecdote of wife-beating.

CHAPTER VIII

THE SYSTEM 131

Influence of the Quran on national life and character. Opposition to schools. Hatred between sects. Whence comes the power of Islam? Hindu and Muslim leagued to 'set back' the world. Impervious to missionary effort. Christian teaching and practice compared. Power of religious tyranny and of faith in the 'divine' Imams. Flagrant perjury. 'Expiation' and 'Taqiya'. Muhammad's 'prudent' teaching. Unity (?) and self-government.

CONTENTS

PART II

POLITICAL SITUATION AND THE FUTURE

CHAPTER I

ENGLAND AND MESOPOTAMIA 153

Past record of Islam. The Anglo-French Declaration. At the Peace Conference. Effect of war *against* Turkey. Appeal to Mecca. The 'Terms'. Muslim intrigues. The Interregnum in Mesopotamia. The revolution. Sir Arnold Wilson and firmness. Sir Percy Scott and the 'Constitution'. Feisal and inefficiency.

CHAPTER II

THE FUTURE 173

Complete, or partial evacuation. Ibn Saud and the Wahabis. Bolshevist propaganda, the fatal danger. Mustapha Kemal. Inevitable return of anarchy. Losses to trade and the taxpayer. Basrah alone, no value. Hopeless weakness of present system. Must create a 'middle class', under British Protectorate. Small land-holdings, direct from Government. Possible development of immense resources, by scientific cultivation. Canals and irrigation. The only way!

APPENDIX

TEXT OF THE ANGLO-FRENCH DECLARATION 191

PART I

THE FAITH AND CUSTOMS OF MESOPOTAMIA

CHAPTER I

THE HOLY CITIES OF SHIA' ISLAM

Life in Najaf. Story of Ali. The 'Holy' men. Orthodox Sunni, unorthodox Shia'. Training and power of the Mujtahid. The city.

HOW MANY OF US in England have heard of the four Holy Cities of the Land of the Two Rivers? How many take into account the effect of their existence on the people whom we discuss so glibly, as though the only difference between them and, say, the inhabitants of Scotland lay in the colour of their skins? Why, in fact, do we so vexatiously persist upon interfering with them, instead of leaving them to their own peaceful and benevolent activities?

The truth remains that these four Holy Cities (holy to the Shia') – Najaf, Kerbela, Kadhimain and Samara – are, *par excellence*, the unique feature of Mesopotamia; and the key to their gates is the key to an understanding of the strength and the weakness of the people.

The essential characteristics of the four are much the same. We will take Najaf, probably the most important, to stand for all four.

Najaf lies about a hundred miles south of Baghdad and six miles from Kufa, the ancient seat of the Imams and the birthplace of the great Islamic split. Leaving the origins of this historic movement to be described later (in Chapter III), it is enough to say here that the Imam Ali (from whose shrine sprang the Holy City), while praying in the Mosque at Kufa, was traitorously set upon and mortally wounded. Making his escape in the confusion which followed, he mounted a camel, and set forth in the darkness into the desert, leaving instructions, however, that he was to be buried on the spot where his body might subsequently be found.

It may be imagined with what diligence the search was carried out the following day. But though every effort was made, no trace of his body could be discovered.

Ali, apparently, was far and away the finest character of all the Imams. At the time of his death he was an old man, noted for his gentleness and sanctity. But his youth and middle age had been resplendent in deeds of martial courage. He had earned the title of The Lion from the Prophet himself, and his unswerving loyalty and utter devotion to his master and teacher render him to any unprejudiced observer a most lovable and inspiring figure. His assassination, naturally, only heightened his reputation, and the pathetic figure of this saintly old man dying alone in the desert soon became the centre of fabulous legends and miraculous tradition. For details as to the growth of the cult of Ali, I must refer my readers to the book of that name, by the Rev. Edward Sell. I would here only emphasise that, having lived for

THE HOLY CITIES OF SHIA' ISLAM

some time in its midst, I found the devotion to Ali among the faithful was most remarkable.

The story runs that many, many years after his assassination the Khaliph Harun al Raschid was hunting near Kufa and became separated from his companions. The deer led him far out into the desert, and at length took refuge in a thicket. When the Khaliph approached he was astonished that, despite every effort, his horse would not or could not enter.

At length the Khaliph was forced to dismount and enter on foot. He found no deer, but in the midst of the thicket there lay the skeletons of a man and a camel.

There remained no doubt in his mind that Allah had led him to the resting-place of Ali, and in accordance with the Imam's dying request, steps were immediately taken for his burial on the spot. Swiftly, and with true Oriental munificence, a shrine was built for the corpse, and over the shrine a magnificent mosque, which formed the nucleus of the teeming city of Najaf as it is today.

West of Kufa the land rises gradually to a height of 120 feet above the river. It then falls away suddenly, thus forming a cliff which runs for many miles across the desert. On the summit of this cliff, overlooking the Arabian desert, stands the city of Najaf. Completely walled in like some grim medieval fortress, dominated by the golden dome of the Shrine of Hadhrat Ali (which is said to be visible from a distance of three days' march), it presents a sight not easily to be forgotten. Except for the surrounding tombs and graves of the faithful in the Wadi a'Salaam, or Valley of Peace, it is

THE INS AND OUTS OF MESOPOTAMIA

self-contained within the walls. No green thing can be seen. Even water for the inhabitants has to be brought three-quarters of a mile, in skins, from the foot of the cliff. To enter it, is to be plunged hundreds of years into the past. Cut off from the world, but an emporium of trade for the desert, its appearance does not belie its character of the Holiest City of the Shia's. It is a turbulent desert town – the seat of religious extravagance and bigotry, of intrigue and turmoil, of oppressive wealth and sanctified poverty, and of a commercial morality and practice unlike any other in the world.

The population of Najaf is estimated at some 45,000 persons, and, as the external circumference of the walls is under three miles, the conditions of overcrowding can be better imagined than described. Moreover, in certain of the great feasts, 120,000 pilgrims pass through its gates. Like some unhealthy sponge, the city sucks and absorbs them, and after three or four days, they are sent forth with empty pockets, to make their way back, as best they may, to far-off Persia, India, the Hedjaz or Palestine.

The Najafis must be divided into two clear classes – the professional religious and the ordinary laymen. It must always be remembered that Najaf is a religious university. The lay Najafi is half Persian and wholly a creature of his environment. Living in an atmosphere of bigotry, often wealthy yet professing poverty, he looks on pilgrims and Badu traders alike as his lawful prey. Isolated, but the receiver and distorter of all the news of the world, which he hears from streams of the faithful always pouring into the Holy City, he

THE HOLY CITIES OF SHIA' ISLAM

exercises a malign influence *far beyond the limits of his town* and even of Iraq. His isolation, and the prestige he claims from those who are forced to visit him in his lair, tend to make him independent, and impatient of reform or control; though as an alien he naturally fears the Arab. The native Arabs are even more independent; and, in their hearts, deeply distrust the Persians.

The merchant of Najaf belongs to a bygone age, when merchandise travelled by caravan through incredible dangers, when the result of a venture was not known for years, and the minimum remuneration was a hundred per cent. The Persian pilgrim, drunk with religious fervour, or the wild Badu, stunned at the sight of a house, are equally at his mercy. He will keep a tin of oil thirty years in his cellars, in the hope that the price will rise a penny, and it would seem that the only hope of commercial progress would be the importation and establishment of a colony of Jews!

Let us now turn to the 'professional' religious. Though, for the sake of clearness, I thus differentiate between the religious and the lay element, yet the whole life, activity, or influence, which radiates from the Holy City, is saturated with what, for want of a better term, must be called Religion. It regulates the people's psychology, it forms and governs their thoughts and acts, it is the ever-present undercurrent of their subconsciousness, and, however apparently remote the aspect we may be endeavouring to understand, we can hear – if we listen for it – the deep rumbling note in the heart of their being.

THE INS AND OUTS OF MESOPOTAMIA

Najaf, as the holiest city of Shia' Islam, is the seat of the great Mujtahidun, who are the real rulers, and therefore merit explanation. A Mujtahid is one who has the power of making an Ijtihad, or 'a logical deduction'. The origin of his authority is thus explained:[1] 'Muhammad wished to send a man named Mu'adh to Yaman to collect alms for distribution among the poor. On appointing him, he said:

' "Oh Mu'adh, by what rule will you act?"

'He replied: "By the Law of the Quran."

' "But if you find no direction therein?"

' "Then I will act according to the Sunnat (or Traditions) of the Prophet."

' "But what if that fails?"

' "Then I will make an ijtihad and act on that."

'The Prophet raised his hands and said: "Praise be to God who guides the messenger of His Prophet in what He pleases."

'This is considered a proof of the authority of Ijtihad, for the Prophet clearly sanctioned it.'

Among the Sunnis, it is practically impossible for anyone to be a Mujtahid. Among the Shia' they not only still exist, but exert an enormous influence on the faithful. The Sunni is compelled to follow the interpretation of the Laws of Islam as laid down by the original founders of the four Schools of Jurisprudence : Hanbali, Shafai, Hanafi, and Malaki, which are for him immutable. The Shia', on the other hand, follows the Laws of the Quran as interpreted by the Imams; and these laws again, or some of them, may, on any emer-

1 From *The Faith of Islam*, by the Rev. Edward Sell, D.D.

gency, be interpreted or modified by the Mujtahidun as they think fit.

He who is for the moment the Chief Mujtahid holds an amazing authority. Here is an interesting example of his power, which at the same time shows how the right to interpret the law is exercised.

The jurist, Shafai, states that tobacco is 'haram' or forbidden, and to this day his 'Sunni' followers never smoke. But there is no mention of tobacco in the Quran, and therefore Shia's are permitted to smoke. It happened some years ago that the Persian Government gave the tobacco monopoly to a Russian company. The Chief Mujtahid of the time, Mirza Hassan Shirazi, residing at Najaf, considered that it was 'haram' to have given this monopoly to 'kafirs' or unbelievers. He therefore issued a fatwah or document bearing the authoritative 'hakamtu' – 'I have decided' – forbidding the use of tobacco by the Shia's in Persia, *and this fatwah was observed*. To anyone who knows the part played by tobacco in Persia, this instant obedience seems nothing short of miraculous! The result was that the Persian Government cancelled the monopoly, and compensated the Russian company. The fatwah was then withdrawn. No Sunni divine could have done this.

It is well known that alcohol is absolutely forbidden. Yet there are many instances where the Mujtahidun have issued fatwahs permitting its use for sick persons for whom, in their opinion, there was no other cure.

Thus the Shia' Mujtahid may interpret the Law; the Sunni may only slavishly follow the Law as it has been interpreted for him.

There purport to be three classes of Mujtahidun, each theoretically in accordance with the standard of knowledge attained. Actually, however, the classification depends on the influence a Mujtahid possesses and the number of his followers.

A Mujtahid can only obtain recognition as such by a certificate from the greatest Mujtahidun. This is usually given for anything up to twenty-five years' study in Najaf under the direct tuition of the great Mujtahidun, to which men of good family seldom care to submit. The examinations are extraordinarily severe and, within the almost limitless limits of the Law, exhaustive. The Rev. Edward Sell mentions the following six requirements for the first degree of Ijtihad.

1. The knowledge of the Quran and all that is related to it: that is to say, a complete knowledge of Arabic literature, a profound acquaintance with the orders of the Quran and all their subdivisions, their relationship to each other and their connection with the orders of the Sunnat. The candidate should know when and why each verse of the Quran was written, he should have a perfect acquaintance with the literal meaning of the words, the speciality or generality of each clause, the abrogating and abrogated sentences. He should be able to make clear the meaning of the obscure passages, to discriminate between the literal and the allegorical, the universal and the particular.

2. He must know the Quran by heart, with all the Traditions and explanations.

THE HOLY CITIES OF SHIA' ISLAM

3. He must have a perfect knowledge of the Traditions or at least three thousand of them. He must know their source, history, object; and their connection with the Laws of the Quran. He should know by heart the most important Traditions.

4. A pious and austere life.

5. A profound knowledge of all the Sciences of the Law.

6. A complete knowledge of the four 'madhhabs' or Schools of Jurisprudence.

Such is the standard of knowledge which, theoretically at all events, is considered necessary at Najaf before anyone can attain to the first degree of Mujtahid. The examinations are both written and oral, and, in accordance with the fourth condition, during the time of his study, no breath of public scandal must have touched the candidate. His life, *coram publico*, must have been blameless and exemplary. The strenuous and lonely life, indeed, can never offer sufficient attraction to tempt any man of good family to forsake the profits of lavish hospitality, and become a Mujtahid.

The next step of the certified Mujtahid is on the death of a great Mujtahid, to gather round himself learned men and send them out to various parts of the world to spread his fame. His influence, if fortune favours, will gather in volume like a snowball, until finally he is recognised by universal acclamation as one of the great Mujtahidun. He will then be addressed by the high-sounding title of *Hujjat al Islam wa'l Muslimin, ayat' ullah fi'l alamin* ('Proof of Islam and of the Muslims, sign of God in the worlds'). How different from the

THE INS AND OUTS OF MESOPOTAMIA

proud title of the Patriarch of Western Christendom, 'Servus servorum Dei!'

There are a certain number of religious learned Shia's commonly, but erroneously, known as Mujtahidun. They are properly 'Muttadaiyin' or pious men, fit to receive charity and to settle minor cases of religious law, but not to decide or issue fatwahs.

It will occasion no surprise if it be said that in such an environment and with so much tradition behind him, the Shia' Mujtahid becomes the veritable incarnation of spiritual and worldly pride. To disobey his command is to incur eternal damnation. He is surrounded by sycophants of the worst type, who echo, one to another, his simplest phrases in admiring modulations. He lives humbly, thus aping the very virtue which his whole arrogant life is spent in violating. He amasses vast sums of money by means which will be dealt with in a subsequent chapter. He never leaves his house save to go to the mosque to pray, and his way is impeded by the hundreds who endeavour to kiss the hem of his garment, or if luck befriend them, his hand. To a few favoured ones he will give a small square of paper on which he has written a verse of the Quran. This, carefully sewn into a small leather wallet, will be worn under the 'araqchin' or skull-cap, or possibly bound on to the arm above the elbow, and is accounted a permanent protection from all the assaults of the devil and his evil spirits. Its power is such that, in the opinion of many, it will ward off physical as well as spiritual danger.

THE HOLY CITIES OF SHIA' ISLAM

Yet – and note this carefully – the Mujtahid will not necessarily have the larger crowd praying behind him in the mosque. For the Shia' prefers to follow in prayer one who is known to be *truly* pious and saintly; and in the House of God mere intellectual efficiency counts for little. For personal communion, the temporal and spiritual authority of the Mujtahid has no weight. The leader in prayer must, so far as possible, be 'ma'sum', i.e. sinless.

It will be seen, however, that to incur the antagonism of a Mujtahid is to find oneself up against an obstacle of vast dimension and almost unlimited power. At the same time, it must not for a moment be imagined that his influence on the general public is direct. They, indeed, are saturated with legalism and the letter of the Law; and the Mutjahid, as the supreme interpreter of the Law, is held in wholesome fear; but they do not hesitate to employ religious rivalry and jealousy between the exalted ones, to their own advantage, showing thereby the vast gulf which exists in their minds between their respect for the office and their opinion of the individual who holds it! There are frequently long discussions among any party preparing to bring a case, as to which Mujtahid or Muttadaiyin it is most prudent to 'go before'; that is, who will decide the case in their favour for the cheapest bribe. Disputes will sometimes hang on interminably, simply because one side refuses to appear before the Mujtahid their opponents have selected. Of course, to approach the Chief Mujtahid with an openly corrupt proposal would be unheard of; but even his supreme power will sometimes be used, without his knowledge, to thwart the ends of justice, as the following incident will show.

Hassan and Ali, merchants of a certain town, were claimant and defendant respectively for the possession of a house. The case was brought before the local Political Officer for decision. The evidence in favour of Ali was overwhelming, and he accordingly remained in possession. Hassan accused Ali of perjury, demanding that he should go to Kerbela to swear on the Shrine of Hussein that his documents and his verbal evidence had been true. Ali was perfectly willing to do so – how, indeed, could he refuse? – and set forth on his journey of about ten days. Having taken the oath, he returned only to find that his house had been burgled and stripped. Hassan at once started the rumour in the bazaar that this was a punishment meted out to Ali by Hussein, *because Ali had perjured himself at his, Hussein's shrine.*

This pious interpretation spread like wildfire; and while Ali was abused by every good Muslim, Hassan was exhorted, by his friends to go at once to the Chief Mujtahid and submit the whole matter to him. This was exactly what Hassan desired, and, accompanied by Ali and the friends of both sides, he set forth. It is hardly necessary to add that His Holiness decided in Hassan's favour. The judgment of the civil court was set aside, Ali was dispossessed, and Hassan, bursting with piety, became the owner of the house.

Outside their own particular line – the Law and all its ramifications – the Mujtahidun are quite incredibly childish. The following incident (told me on unimpeachable authority) occurred not very long ago. The Killidar (treasurer) of a certain well-known shrine in Persia came to visit Kerbela on pilgrimage. His official position had involved the duty of host to all pilgrims from Kerbela who had visited this shrine, and he had earned their gratitude by his hospitality, kindliness, and generosity. Now, it is the custom among the Sufis (or Mystics) to wear long moustaches and, though he was not a Sufi, yet the length of his moustache tempted the student element of Kerbela to spread the rumour that their Holy City was being defiled by the presence of this most hated and damnable sect. At this time the Chief Mujtahid was in residence at Kerbela, and they went to him and told him the awful news. He immediately wrote a letter to the offender, of whom he knew nothing personally, and forbade him absolutely to enter the shrine. The Killidar was not unnaturally furious at this insult and plainly asked His Holiness what he meant by wantonly insulting one who had so liberally entertained many thousands of the Kerbelais, to be now rewarded by this outrageous behaviour. Letters of explanation and apology followed, but the students were still not pacified. The Chief Mujtahid, therefore, at last told the Killidar that there would be no objection to his visiting the shrine if he would first cut down his moustache! The reply was, 'Remove first your beard!'

I have said above that it is from the Holy Cities, as great nerve-centres, that there radiates an active religious force which permeates the tribesmen. I have tried to describe the centre of these ganglia. But it must be kept in mind that the Mujtahid is himself moulded by the people. He has gained his position, partly by learning, but more by popularity, which must at all costs be retained. The same policy actuates those immediately below him in the Hierarchy – the Ulema – or the 'learned'. These are ancient men whose degree of sanctity or of importance is advertised by the size of their head-dress, a vast turban. I have been informed – and I have every reason to believe it – that in the days of the Turkish Government, these immense turbans were used as convenient receptacles for revolvers and ammunition or other weapons of offence. The Mujtahid maintains his authority through the Ulema; and they, in their turn, depend on the influence of their clientele. The latter are primarily students, and, secondarily, the general public. All Holy Cities are centres of learning. Being also the centres of religion, the educational policy is that the end-all and be-all of learning is religious knowledge. Reading and writing are only taught that they may be of use in questions of religion. The student should be able to read the Quran and make copies of religious works, or write them. Calligraphy is considered a fine art; and reasonably enough, since the language of these people is supposed to be the mother-tongue of the inhabitants of Heaven! Much time is devoted to the subject, and some of the religious leaders write a wonderfully beautiful hand. Thereby they gain much kudos and respect.

Najaf is the most important of these universities. There are about twenty colleges, which contain about 6,000 students. Owing to the fact that the Shia' Mujtahid is allowed to place his own interpretation on the Law, on the Traditions, and on the sayings of the Imams, the study of Shia' Religious Law has practically no limits. It is truly a very comprehensive and complicated study. The elementary stages include the Law of Divorce and Inheritance, and the Levitical Law of 'ayun bil ayun' and 'sin bil sin' – an eye for an eye and a tooth for a tooth – all of which must be mastered by the would-be Mujtahid at a comparatively early stage in his career. This encourages to an astonishing degree the power and the love of splitting hairs. For example, the Quran ordains that the hands of robbers are to be cut off. Whether the amputation should be from the knuckles, wrist, elbow or shoulder is left to the Mujtahid to decide. There has been much controversy upon this question, which has provided material for many volumes that must be studied with care.

The large number of students at Najaf – ranging in age from fourteen to sixty and even over – is due to the many advantages attaching to graduation thereat. Firstly, no fees are required, but sufficient money is given to students from charities to maintain themselves *and their families*. Their allowances are not conditional on continued application to study. It is almost unbelievable, but none the less a fact, that many of the students have enjoyed a comparatively comfortable income and free quarters for thirty or forty years without having mastered the art of reading and writing.

Though the colleges are all residential, yet a very large number of students live in the city, attending their lectures daily. Thus it is that the influence of the colleges permeates the whole atmosphere and radiates to the surrounding country.

It is inevitable that only an infinitesimal number of students ever attain to any position of importance in the religious world, and though such an easy life is obviously attractive, it does not lead to anything that could be called a career. On the other hand, the average student is, in many ways, well rewarded for his labour. First there is the position he holds in the family circle and among his less fortunate friends – no small thing in his eyes. A more practical outcome will be 'letters' from his lecturers, from some Alim, or even from a Mujtahid, which recommend him as a suitable person to handle or receive charities – a most lucrative employment! – or give him authority to decide on minor religious disputes, which is equally advantageous. But there are many who fail to make any advance in learning, and others who tire of the road to knowledge and the strict religious life. These become 'qaris' or readers of the Quran.

In the Wadi a'Salaam, outside the walls of the Holy City, sleep kings' ministers, nobles and merchants, the rich and the poor; and over their graves the reader reads verses of the Quran and trims the lights to keep off the lover of darkness. A visit to the Wadi on a Thursday evening will reveal over two thousand of these men engaged in earning their pious livelihood. The emoluments are not high, but in addition they are enrolled on the list of Holy Poor, and receive their share in the general distribution of alms made monthly by the Chief Mujtahid.

THE HOLY CITIES OF SHIA' ISLAM

It is the prevailing mental atmosphere that I have tried to outline above, which is common to all the Holy Cities. We may now turn to the conditions of living, to gain an accurate view of the environment which goes to make up the character of the inhabitants. Here again the description of one city will be, in essentials, true of all.

Najaf today consists of a cramped town of narrow streets and rickety houses, surrounding a magnificent mosque. The majority of the streets are not much more than eight feet wide, and many are much narrower. I have frequently been squashed up against a wall to make room for a donkey which was carrying two water-skins, one on each side.

The lattice windows project from the sides of the houses, often overlapping each other and completely shutting out both sun and air. Leading up to the mosque is a broad and well-covered bazaar. In Najaf this is about a quarter of a mile in length. There is one unique feature in this city. Each house contains at least one tier of cellars. Being built on the top of a cliff, there is no limit to the depth of the houses, and it is natural to take refuge from the heat by going underground. The larger buildings contain three, four, or even five tiers of cellars or, as they are called, 'siradib', the singular of which is 'sirdab'. Their practical value is shown by the fact that when the temperature above ground is 125 degrees in the shade, it is advisable to wear an overcoat three flights below! Many of these houses inter-communicate through their cellars, offering the means for crime before which our civilised imagination can only shudder.

THE INS AND OUTS OF MESOPOTAMIA

Their presence, indeed, has gone far to support the richly deserved reputation of Najaf as the wickedest and most corrupt city of Iraq – a reputation which even the faithful Shia' admit.

Each house also contains a well, more than a hundred feet deep, of water which is foul to the taste, and brings on a form of dysentery. The house will also probably contain one or two tombs, and the sanitation is primitive in the extreme.

The roads and buildings all rise from the insecure foundation of these crumbling and rotting 'siradib', into which percolates the refuse of the whole city.

This great sponge, saturated with the slime of dormant sickness, is shut in on all sides by the wall mentioned above. That it has not hitherto been visited by an annihilating disease is a matter for surprise, but it does not seem possible it can be long delayed.

Such, then, is a very brief sketch of a Holy City, the directing force of the life of thousands. Only a bare outline has been attempted, so that the reader may be able to fill in at his leisure the details which I hope to describe subsequently.

CHAPTER II

SHIA' OBLIGATIONS

How religion rules their whole life. Stories of the prevailing avarice. The obligation, and the profits, of charity. Tyranny of the 'Holy'.

IN DEALING WITH any race of people as a whole it is often not practicable to label them with any one predominant vice or virtue. As a rule, so many elements enter into their general psychology, so many interests and influences are brought to bear upon them, that their reactions to these present a kaleidoscope of qualities, of which one stands out at one time and one at another. This is not so with the Arabs of Mesopotamia, mainly, I think, because the influence which predominates in their whole life is *one* – their Religion. And yet it is also true that as a whole they are irreligious. This appears to be a paradox, but in reality the one influence leads naturally to the opposite effect.

Primarily their religion is ever with them. There is no division in their mind between civil and religious matters. All questions are settled before the Mujtahidun or the Ulema. Personal quarrels, when not decided by knife or rifle, are settled by an oath on the Shrine of Hussein or

THE INS AND OUTS OF MESOPOTAMIA

Abbas at Kerbela, or of Ali at Najaf, whose names are for ever on their lips in ordinary conversation. The very supports and cross-pieces of the desert house made of reeds are odd in number, so that the total, when divided by two, will leave one, the symbol of God's unity. There is no activity of their daily life in its ordinary routine that has not been regulated by tradition or the Quran. In short, their conduct, within clearly defined and unbreakable barriers, is absolutely regulated by 'the Law' – no whit different in fact from that of the Jews before the Incarnation. Indeed, an understanding of the life of the Old Testament Jew is an excellent guide to the psychology of the Arab.

It may be expected therefore that this common motive will react along certain very definite lines. Bound within rigid limits, the weakness of the human character is likewise limited in its manifestations, and we may look for a predominant vice or virtue, common to all. As regards the former we find it in Pride, which manifests itself practically as Avarice. Having adjudged cases in the Criminal Court of Baghdad for a year, sitting daily for at least five hours, I cannot remember any case which had not this vice as its motive force. Deliberate infliction of pain for pain's sake I never came across. It was rare that mutual stabbings came before me as the outcome of a simple quarrel. In every case of the sort which I recall at the moment, the dispute was over some small debt, a piece of ground, or the dowry of a wife.

That this vice is not a modern development can be seen from Arabic literature. The *Thousand and One Nights* are full of extravagant praise for one

SHIA' OBLIGATIONS

who is generous, and to this day an open-handed charity excites the greatest wonder and admiration. One who spends much money on the gratification of his own pleasures is openly regarded as an imbecile – and the meanest and most vile methods are sometimes employed to obtain such gratification as cheaply as possible. The size of the 'madhif' – or the place set apart for the entertainment of guests – is an index of greatness, and the amount of people entertained and the costliness of the banquet, are all well advertised to the glory of the host. It is not, however, generally known that every one of his 'fellaliyeh' has to pay in to the Sheikh a certain amount of tribute in kind, and that the much-advertised feast actually costs the Sheikh himself little or nothing!

Among the tribes, brother will fight against brother over the question of a small canal. Each will bring forth his own retainers and friends, and they will have a hearty set-to with daggers or clubs as weapons. The original quarrel probably arose over the action of one brother in damming up the water so as to divert it on to his land, and not removing the dam at the promised time, thereby depriving the other brother of his rightful share and endangering his crop. If, in the ensuing quarrel, anyone is accidentally killed, the matter will be settled by 'fasl', or blood-money. Each tribe has its price laid down for a man or a horse, and it is very rarely that a tribal murder is brought before the Civil Government to settle, for no money could be made out of it. The question of 'fasl' even extends to dogs. Every little colony of Arabs has innumerable dogs which belong to no

THE INS AND OUTS OF MESOPOTAMIA

one, and which wander about the village eating garbage and refuse. They are, however, exceedingly useful as watchdogs, and as such have their value in Arab eyes. The 'fasl' payable in their case is as much grain as will cover the corpse of the dog when it is stretched out. It is surprising, when the grain is rice, how much it takes to cover the animal completely!

But if this vice of avarice is common among the tribes, it is far more so in the cities, and above all in the Holy Cities. Here the end-all and be-all of existence is the extraction of money from the unwary. From the highest to the lowest there runs a vast network, an incredible organisation, through which those in authority may reap a rich and unending harvest. The mainspring of this organisation is the Shia' charities. I desire to put the matter as fairly as possible, and it will be evident that I am only too anxious to give credit where credit is due, but the abuses which are perpetrated under the guise of religion are too utterly blatant to escape notice, and are obvious to the faithful themselves, who have many times mentioned them to me.

The population of the Holy Cities is – whether necessarily or not – largely supported by charities or by payment for special religious services rendered. It is this which, above all, makes the atmosphere so depressing. The two motives of (a) money for the sake of power, and (b) power for the sake of money actuate every moment of the lives of ninety per cent of the inhabitants. The jealousy and rivalry among the religious leaders never cease. There is no mutual trust between any of them.

SHIA' OBLIGATIONS

Each one is concerned only in trying to increase his own reputation for learning and sanctity, in order that his pockets may be well filled. One of the most revolting sights that I ever saw was at a distribution of the Oudh Bequest in Najaf.

This is a large sum of money which was left by the Royal House of Oudh in India, from which the interest is distributed every three months to the poor of the Holy Cities of Najaf and Kerbela. In Islam, those who distribute charities have to be paid. In this case there are six of the Ulema who are appointed distributors, though of course they do nothing, the whole work being carried out by the British Government. In the time of the Turks, the British Consul at Baghdad supervised the business. One year the work fell into my hands. The distribution took place in the house of one of the Ulema. The Holy Men squatted on their heels at one end of the verandah, fondling and smoothing their long grey beards, each with a perpetual smile of supreme self-satisfaction. Not one of them but had ample means to live in comparative comfort. The verandah was slightly raised, and in the courtyard outside was a mob which made one almost physically sick to look upon, while the arising odour remains in my imagination to this day. They were mostly women, all veiled and the majority diseased. In the vain hope that they would get more than had been previously determined, they would expose their maimed and mangled bodies. Some had no hands, others were legless and propelled themselves along like grotesque beetles. One old woman tried to drag herself up the steps on to the verandah, and fell back. She was para-

THE INS AND OUTS OF MESOPOTAMIA

lysed, and it remains a mystery to this day how she ever reached the house. Another had no face and, as she withdrew her veil and exposed her deformity, it was as much as I could do not to shriek. All were painfully emaciated, many of them actually starving. The amount that they received was in many cases only three rupees. Some, more fortunate, had larger sums, but these were mostly young, healthy students in the colleges, who had been included in the list of the Holy Poor through favour of the Ulema. The Holy Men who were present received anything from three hundred rupees each. The Chief Mujtahid himself, I believe, should have received five hundred or a thousand, I am not certain which, but he would not accept it. He of course was not present. I examined a list of the recipients afterwards, and found that one of the 'holy' distributors had included in the list no less than twenty-five of his own relations.

Abuses like this are perfectly well known to the general public, but they are accepted without demur. The iron hold of formalism is nowhere more obvious than in the Holy Cities. The people have no delusions as to the real characters of their Mujtahidun and Ulema. It is almost nauseating to hear the common folk in the city, or from the surrounding tribes, discussing which of the Ulema shall hear their case – in other words, weighing up their own chances against the length of their opponents' purse.

And yet there is no hesitation about paying the Zakat, or the Khums, or the contribution for lighting the shrine, and the distributing of water, or

SHIA' OBLIGATIONS

the Hissat Imam, which is money handed over to make provision for the promised Mahdi.

Almsgiving is one of the practical obligations of Islam, and Zakat is a legal tithe paid by every Muslim. It was originally the general tax for the upkeep of the Prophet's establishment and the organisation of the conquered territory. It was laid down in the Quran, and the conditions of its payment carefully defined. It is only obligatory if the payee be a Muslim free man, and has the wherewithal to pay. Zakat is levied on goods in kind as well as on actual cash, also on cattle and other herds. It is laid down to whom Zakat must be paid, and for what purpose it may be employed.

Alms are to be given to the poor and needy, and to those who collect them, and for ransoms and for debtors *and for the cause of God*, and for wayfarers.

It will at once be noticed that a very wide interpretation may be placed on the italicised words.

Further, it must be borne in mind that the 'poor and needy' are those who choose to live in poverty. It is therefore not unusual for a wealthy person to be in a perpetual state of uncertainty as to whether he shall advertise his wealth and gain immediate power and prestige, or conceal it and thereby acquire more.

The deep-rooted hatred felt by even wealthy men at having to part with their money is well shown in the following incident. A hospital was erected at Najaf, and became most popular. Its wards were always full, and the out-patients' department was crowded every morning and evening. To help in its upkeep, and reduce the attendance to manageable proportions, it was decided to ask a small fee from those who could afford it. The charge to out-patients was fourpence, and those who paid were to be attended before the free patients, for whom a bench was provided while they were waiting. One morning the Civil Surgeon was not a little astonished to find the Killidar of Najaf, together with his uncle the Naqib al Ashraf, seated on the free bench. These two were the wealthiest persons in the town, and in our currency would probably be worth anything up to ten thousand pounds a year. They preferred the humiliation of classing themselves with the beggars of the city to parting with fourpence!

Zakat is one of the three main divisions of the general duty of alms to the poor. The whole of these alms must be paid to a Mujtahid, or the donor acquires little merit. Further, the greater the Mujtahid the more acceptable and meritorious the sacrifice. No receipt is given, and there is no such thing as a regular statement of accounts. It is not difficult to understand the desire to become a great Mujtahid.

It would be difficult to assess the total sum that annually flows in to the Chief Mujtahid's private purse. But bearing in mind the above facts, and that contributions are sent from all over the world, it must be colossal. A few years ago much scandal was caused to the faithful on the death of a very great Mujtahid indeed. He had passed his life in the simplest possible manner. A threadbare carpet had covered his floor and only the barest necessities in the way of furniture could be seen. He had

SHIA' OBLIGATIONS

not been long in his grave before it was discovered that he had purchased a large portion of land in a neighbouring, most prosperous, town, and built thereon a large bazaar, the rentals from which would keep his family in affluence *in perpetuo*. Still, so elastic is the conscience of the devout Muslim, or perhaps it would be more accurate to say so hide-bound is he in his respect for tradition, that it caused no more than a passing scare, and the matter was shortly forgotten.

The other two divisions of alms for the poor are the Khums and the Radd Mazalim. The former, as its name denotes, is the fifth part of the income and the perquisite of poor Syeds or descendants of the Prophet. These literally swarm in the Holy Cities and are treated with the utmost respect. Their green turbans are to be seen everywhere. Many of them are merchants. Here again one may notice a curious anomaly in the psychology of the people. It is public knowledge that some unscrupulous persons, suddenly and without any kind of claim, adopt the title of Syed, and appear in the green turban. Though the lie is palpable to the meanest intelligence, no one ever disputes their pretensions. The most flagrant case that occurs to me was that of a Burmese who came over with a British Officer as his cook. This officer died, and the Burmese decided to marry and remain in the country. He duly made the profession of faith, and within a month was being addressed as Syed Ali!

The Radd Mazalim requires a little explanation. Salaries to Government officials and servants are necessarily paid out of taxes exacted from the people by Law, in addition to what they already pay as Zakat to the Religious Hierarchy. To the strict Shia' therefore it is 'haram' to accept such salaries. It is, however, possible to enjoy the fruits of labour without transgression by the purchase of special forgiveness from a Mujtahid.

These three divisions, then, are obligatory – the Zakat and the Khums on all whose state of life fulfils the above-mentioned conditions, the Radd Mazalim on all Government employees.

Money for the distribution of water is not an obligation, but such a gift is an act of great merit. This, too, must be paid to one of the Mujtahidun. Another most important charity is for the lighting of the shrine. The sum provided is also used for the upkeep of the private sepulchres of Shia' families, and it is from this fund that the Qaris referred to in the last chapter are paid. This money is in the control of the Killidar or Treasurer of the Shrine, a family appointment descending from father to son. He need be neither a Mujtahid nor an Alim. It is estimated that at Najaf he receives at least £10,000 annually for the lighting of the shrine alone. In addition to the above, there are miscellaneous sums of a more or less voluntary nature which are handed over to the great Ulema, as, for example, fees paid in return for an order that prayers and fastings on behalf of a certain person – generally deceased – be observed for periods that vary according to the amount paid. Another voluntary contribution is money vowed to big Ulema in return for recovery from sickness or extrication from danger.

There are many other means whereby money finds its way into the possession of the Hierarchy.

SHIA' OBLIGATIONS

Those which I have already mentioned do not of course include the small contributions paid by the faithful on great feast-days or at the ordinary Friday prayer-meetings in the mosque. An important feast will see no less than 120,000 pilgrims pouring into Najaf or Kerbela. The sum taken at such times must be very large.

I can think of no stronger proof of the astonishing power of Islam over the people than that which I have set forth above. On the one hand we have a people whose one desire above all desires is to amass money by fair means or foul, whose besetting sin is avarice to a degree that we in the West can hardly imagine, to whom ordinary generosity is so remarkable a virtue that it is recorded in their literature. Yet, knowing – as they do know perfectly well – the ultimate destination of the larger proportion of this so prized and hardly earned money that they hand over, they give it without a murmur of discontent or reproach. At the word of authority, their omnipresent vice becomes non-existent, their inborn instinct becomes atrophied, their normal point of view reversed.

It is, I repeat, more than astonishing that this particular practical obligation of almsgiving should be so scrupulously fulfilled, when prayer is almost totally neglected. It would be thought that prayer would be far easier for them, and the effort necessary to learn the ceremonial and the words far less distressing, and as a fact this is so. But the explanation is not far to seek. In spite of their exalted position in the religious life the Mujtahidun and the Ulema are not overmuch concerned with the spiritual progress of their flock. They care little for the spiritual life of the faithful – the life that is nourished by prayer and fasting – but they are very much concerned with their own material life, and woe betide the unfortunate who, by means of one of their innumerable sycophants, is found to be neglectful of this most practical and necessary duty of almsgiving. Such a neglect will react at once on the sycophant himself, and the close-fisted one will very soon be brought to book.

It will at once be remarked that these three duties of the Muslim – prayer, fasting, and almsgiving – are the same as those of the Christian, though we seldom find the same command issuing from our Lord and the Prophet Muhammad. Is there any question at all as to who obtains the greater obedience? Who prays the most, the Muslim or the Christian? Does the Christian keep his Lent with the same whole-hearted obedience as the Muslim his Ramadhan? Is there any doubt about which of the two gives the more in alms? And yet there are many who despise the Muslim, flattering themselves with their own superiority as Christians. There is an Arabic proverb which is indeed applicable: 'God knows, and Time will show.'

I have dwelt upon this question of Shia' charities as, for my purpose, it is very important. It bears with great significance on the nature of the people and their leaders.

We see the immense weakness of character produced by a hard-and-fast formalism. Before the will of their traditional religious leaders they are helpless, and yet in other ways the Arab of Iraq is

SHIA' OBLIGATIONS

a magnificent specimen. Sheikhs of tribes, absolute masters of thousands of fighting men, and masters not merely by birth but by character and personality, are utterly incapable of raising a finger against the gross extortion to which they are subject. It is not as if they did not know that the greater proportion of their contributions remains in the coffers of the Mujtahidun and Ulema. Not only do they know, but they know that their people know. They have told me so in the privacy of my study more than once. At the time of the scandal referred to above, when the Chief Mujtahid was found to have purchased valuable land, a very well-known and respected Syed said to me: 'Your Government is paying much too much respect to the Ulema. The whole country is groaning under their extortions, and now is the time when their system has been exposed by this scandal. Only let the Government act quickly, for the Arab soon forgets.' Which was exactly what happened.

The people are helpless to protest. Any diminution of the accustomed quota would cause endless trouble, and indeed might even involve the loss of the Sheikh's position, which depends to a large extent on the support of the tribesmen, whose ignorance and superstition would easily be utilised by the professional religious for the carrying out of their designs. At the same time this chapter will, I hope, show the willingness of the Arab to submit to religious discipline. An emotional race requires some practical outlet to express itself, and it is this which, in their religious life, the duty of almsgiving largely supplies. The external expression of their faith is stern and simple. The ritual of

THE INS AND OUTS OF MESOPOTAMIA

their daily prayers is the ritual of the Friday service in the mosque. Their 'ornament' is a prayer carpet. But they love to give free vent to their emotional life on any occasion that provides the opportunity. It is this generosity of temperament that is so exploited by the Mujtahidun and Ulema, and which, directed into other channels, would be of great value.

But, which is of greater importance, we have seen in this chapter the real spirit of the Holy Cities — the *leit-motif* of the Hierarchy — their tenderest spot, the joint in their armour. There are very, very few among the town and riverain Arabs who are religious in the Western sense of the word. But if they can be induced to think that their faith is being attacked, they become exceedingly religious in the Oriental sense! Those in more important positions and better educated are naturally harder to move, but the Ulema would leave these to be played upon by their dependants, and themselves deal with the more ignorant and superstitious. Hardly any Arab is brave enough to risk his popularity and thereby his emoluments; for he is in the grip of an organisation against which rebellion would not only be futile, but which would almost certainly destroy him, body and soul.

CHAPTER III

MUHARRAM

The obligation of penance. The martyrdom of Hussein. Head-cutting and breast-beating. The 'merit' of suffering.

THE DESIRE TO EXPRESS religious convictions by external observance is well shown during the first ten days of the month of Muharram[1] and during the month of Ramadhan.

It may be wondered why, as was stated earlier, the daily duty of prayer is so neglected. For in this we have a mass of detailed private ritual which, it would be thought, would provide ample opportunity for any such expression. The answer lies in two important conditions.

Firstly, the great majority do not know the actual words of the necessary prayers; and anything like extempore prayer is unheard of. The prostrations and manual acts have to be done with the most minute degree of exactitude, and not more than five per cent of the few who have received this detailed instruction ever remember it. It is far better for them to give up prayer altogether than

---

[1] The Sunni only observe the tenth day of the month.

THE INS AND OUTS OF MESOPOTAMIA

lay themselves open to all sorts of heresy and blasphemy, by making some mistake.

Though a few – very few – Muslims know certain parts of the Quran by heart, there is nothing like a systematic religious instruction except in the colleges at Najaf or Kerbela. In each village there is generally a small mosque, in charge of a Mullah who is usually painfully ignorant himself. A few village children may attend until they are bored, which almost always occurs within the year. The knowledge that they acquire during this time will be the sum total of their religious training for the whole of their lives.

But perhaps daily prayer is chiefly neglected because it is a private and solitary affair. The Shia' of Iraq is a gregarious person. He likes a crowd. Loneliness is abhorrent to him. This is, of course, the survival of the tribal instinct when he was a wanderer in the desert, the true Nomad. Those who never say the prescribed daily prayers themselves will, when near a mosque, frequently attend the Friday service therein and join in the common worship, where no mental effort is required. The people are as a whole incredibly lazy thinkers, and their ignorance of their own faith is, as a general rule, abysmal. But in the mosque they will only have to follow the man in front in his prostrations; mistakes are not likely to occur, and in any case would not be noticeable in the crowd. Finally, their mere presence will give them much prestige.

Their intensely strong emotional life finds full outlet during the first ten days of Muharram. Much has been written of this, but nothing, I

MUHARRAM

think, of the actual observances at the fountain-head of the Shia' sect, the Shrine of Ali at Najaf.

Muharram is the first month of the Muslim year, and the tenth day is most holy for all Islam, for on it God created 'Adam and Eve, His Throne, Heaven, Hell, the Seat of Judgment, the Tablet of Decree, the Pen, Fate, Life and Death'.[1] The observance of the first nine days, however, is peculiar to the Shia', and this annual event keeps at fever heat the animosity and hatred between them and the Sunni. It is with the Shia', the commemoration of the martyrdom of Hussein and his companions on the battlefield of Kerbela, which took place as follows.

After the murder of Ali at Kufa referred to above, his eldest son, Hasan, would normally have become Khalif; but he renounced his claim and took an oath of allegiance to Muawiyah, who was to all intents and purposes the murderer of his father. This Muawiyah was an exceedingly able man, and having now become Khalif, was determined that his son Yazid should succeed him. It is said by the Shia' that he contrived to have Hasan poisoned, but in any case his only rival died under peculiar circumstances most conveniently for his plans. Yazid eventually succeeded, but soon proved himself the reverse of the Muslim ideal. He openly patronised every vice, and was himself a drunkard and profligate. The people of Kufa were much scandalised, and sent for Hussein, the brother of Hasan, to seize the Khaliphate from the house of Muawiyah. Trusting in the power of his name and

---

[1] Sell, *Faith of Islam*.

parentage, believing in the protestations of loyalty from the men of Kufa, he and his family set out from Mecca with a hundred foot-soldiers and forty cavalry. He was met by three thousand men on the plains of Kerbela, and no assistance was forthcoming from Kufa. His little force was thus cut off from water, and, naturally, was slowly reduced. Tradition tells us, however, that they held out for three days, until only Hussein and his young son were left alive. But the enemy seemed to have hesitated before such determined resistance from the little band, and superstition held them back from attacking the son of Ali. At last an arrow pierced the ear of the child, and the spell was broken. They rushed upon Hussein and cut him to pieces, carrying away his head as a proof of his death.

For several weeks before the actual month of commemoration of the tragedy, bodies of men and boys about a hundred strong form themselves into bands under a chosen leader. Each band specialises in some particular form of physical asceticism. Some are composed of breast-beaters, others scourge their backs with chains. It is generally believed, though not officially laid down, that by taking an active part in these observances the faithful obtain a plenary absolution for all sins of commission or omission committed during the past year. The Ulema stoutly deny this, though they admit that such action is meritorious. But those who take part – the ordinary folk – are convinced that their souls are wholly purged. This largely accounts for the intense desire of the choicest black-

MUHARRAM

guards to take their share in this self-inflicted mortification!

Before describing these ceremonies in detail, let me try to explain what seems to be the psychology of the people at this time. Their emotions are stirred to a high pitch, but they have no 'sense of sin', as we understand it. As the culminating tenth day approaches they grow more and more excited. The work in Government offices becomes steadily less efficient. They are keyed up, bursting with something they cannot analyse. Often the men have come to me for a day's leave, that they may join the head-cutting procession. Far from showing signs of grief, they have been wild with the joy of anticipation – the anticipation of a real emotional orgy. The event they are celebrating is not, until the actual moment, by any means uppermost in their minds. Happiness and joy in life are never more evident in their ordinary conduct than during these days.

I remember one instance which is typical. On the fifth evening of Muharram I was talking to a young Arab of about eighteen years old. He was far in advance of the average in intelligence, but, as a rule, languid and torpid. This particular evening he was one scintillating mass of exuberance – amusing and witty. We went out together to a large village about three miles off, climbing to the roof of a house from which to see one of the processions, which soon after stopped just below us. A small boy stood up and recited the story of the battle of Kerbela. The dead silence of the crowd, the deep night-sky of the tropics, the soft waving of the palms in the background, and the childish voice telling a story that to any ears is tragic in the extreme, all made up a picture that I shall never forget. Suddenly my companion collapsed. He sank to his knees, his head buried in his arms, leaning against the parapet, sobbing as though his heart would break. There could be no doubt as to the genuineness of his grief. I could never have believed that an Arab could show such depth of genuine emotion. It could not have been done for effect, to impress the crowd, as we were alone on the roof. I walked a little away from that sobbing figure, until the procession had passed on and he came across to me. I could detect no sign of any lasting effect. As we walked back he was once more as gay and voluble as he had been earlier in the evening. He told me that he was always affected in that way by hearing the story, and gave me some further details of the tradition with completely restored cheerfulness.

Again, if on the night of the tenth an unbeliever happens to meet the procession of the head-cutters, each armed with a murderous-looking sword and calling upon Ali, Hasan, and Hussein, he will be greeted with a friendly smile. The general attitude may be summed up in the words, 'God's in His Heaven, all's right with the world.' But at the actual time of the performance of any mortification it is well for the 'kafir' (i.e. unbeliever) to keep clear, or – if he be well known to the performers – to preserve an attitude of reverential and respectful sympathy. For the emotion of the moment is genuine and true – an expression of utter devotion and loyalty to Ali and his sons, Hasan and Hussein. I am not prepared to say whether it is the

MUHARRAM

same of all Islam, but as to the Iraqi there is no manner of doubt that his whole phenomenal life is one kaleidoscope of changing emotions – uncontrolled and, while they last, absolutely sincere. I will return, however, to the actual ceremonies.

The bands already mentioned are all carefully drilled. For example, the beating of the chest must be done in a special way. Both arms are flung up to their full extent and then allowed to fall almost limp. As they pass the chest they strike it with the hands, and then the arms fall to the side. Each band is accompanied by a boy 'reader' of about fourteen years old, who has been chosen for his skill in elocution. It is his duty to read or recite to the band, pausing at every ten or twelve words – when the blows must be heard; so that he plays the part of conductor. The bands of breast-beaters are the most numerous: one is composed entirely of 'Servants of the Shrine' – all Syeds – the others admit the lowest strata of the city to their ranks. The Syed band numbers about two hundred and fifty persons. Each band forms a kind of choir, for, wherever it stops, the masses flock round and in their turn begin beating their breasts, led by the trained band. The sound produced is quite unique and curiously threatening and uncanny. On a still night I have heard the dull thud of the breast-beating in Najaf, from a point in the desert over three miles distant.

It must be realised that these ceremonies do really involve a great capacity for endurance. Self-sufficient and inobservant Europeans often declare that it is all done for show, and that there is no real pain attached. They clearly overlook, or forget, that the mortification is practised at least twenty times nightly for ten nights in succession; that whenever the band stops each man strikes himself not less than a hundred times, and that each blow must fall on exactly the same spot. As a matter of fact, many of these men's chests present a ghastly sight on the tenth day.

To acquire the knack of back-beating with chains is more difficult. Three chains nearly a third of an inch thick and about fourteen inches long are fastened together at one end, and grasped in the right hand. Then the arm is flung up to its full height, and the chain allowed to fall over the head, striking between the shoulder-blades. No force beyond the actual weight of the chain is used at first, until near the close of the ten days, as strength to endure to the end must be preserved, though, on the other hand, the final blows are often delivered with the man's whole strength. Every band, whether of back- or chest-beaters, is accompanied by its Reader, its Torches – in large braziers carried on poles, its Banners – among which that of Ali[1] is conspicuous, and a motley crowd, who contribute to the illuminations by carrying household lamps. They are joined by musicians and others whose business it is to make as much noise as possible on instruments it would be hard to identify.

The climax comes on the morning of the tenth day with the head-cutting. In Najaf, which is full of Persians, this ceremony is largely confined to

[1] An open hand on a stick, the fingers representing the five members of the Prophet's family – Muhammad, Fatima, Ali, Hasan, and Hussein.

MUHARRAM

them, more particularly to the Turkoman tribe, the cruellest race of a cruel people. For ten days they adopt every conceivable device for working themselves up to a pitch of frenzy, tenderly nursing their swords and vying with each other in sharpening them. They are to be met occasionally parading the town with their own peculiar 'sideways' step: the long line of perhaps two hundred and fifty men, each holding on to his neighbour with his left hand, the right hand grasping the sword, shouting in unison, 'Hasan, Hussein, Ali! — Ali, Hasan, Hussein!'

As they march, the right foot is placed in front of the left, the left takes a pace to the left, and the right repeats the first movement. With the movement of the right foot, the right hand swings the sword across the body to the left, the point upwards. As the left foot makes its step, the hand swings back, and as the right foot comes forward once more the sword is brought across the body and upwards, as though to cut the head with an upward movement.

This slow progress is regularly maintained through the narrow and tortuous streets of the city during the four or five nights immediately preceding the tenth.

On the ninth of Muharram, yards and yards of new white linen or cotton are bought and made up into long robes which come down to the feet. It was the custom in the Holy Cities and in the villages around to approach the representative of Government for money to purchase this material. During the Turkish regime, the motive underlying this was probably some subtle desire to force the hated

Sunni into vicarious participation in the commemoration of those who were martyred by his detestable forebears. But under British rule, I can only imagine that it was the desire to save money at the expense of the 'kafir'. And yet, on the evening before the tenth a crowd of at least a thousand persons came and formed up outside my office, in all the picturesque panoply of their ceremonial, and prayed for me, led by their Raudha Khan or preacher, while all the crowd responded, 'Amin, amin, amin.'

I confess to being not a little touched.

However, we will return to our Turkomans. Having procured their white garments and completely shaved their heads, they pass the whole night in the coffee shops, sharpening their swords, eating vast quantities of dates, and drinking an incredible amount of tea, in order, as I was informed, to raise the blood-pressure. At about 6 a.m. they all forgather at the shrine, and there, discarding their ordinary dress, they put on the new white grave-clothes. Sword in hand, they form up into a large circle in the vast outer court of the mosque, each one linked to his neighbour and all facing inwards. In the centre of the circle stands the leader, whose passionate exhortations are skilfully directed to work them up to the necessary pitch of enthusiasm.

Under the guidance of this leader, the circle will begin to move round, ever faster and faster. He watches for the psychological moment; and suddenly, with a shriek of 'Sheikhsan' (Sheikh Hussein) be brings his sword down on his own head. The blood spurts up and falls, covering his white

MUHARRAM

robe with a crimson stain. The sight of the blood removes all restraint and all order. Shouts of 'Hasan, Hussein, Ali!' and the dull blow of the swords mingle with the shrieks, groans, and sobs of the onlookers.

Then, forming in pairs, this ghastly band leaves the mosque and proceeds round the town, slashing themselves every few yards. As their frenzy mounts, so they grow wilder in their actions, drawing the swords across their breasts, which they have bared by tearing their robes, that are by this time no more than dripping masses of blood. Blood is everywhere – in the gutters and splashed on the walls of the houses. The roof of every house is crowded with spectators as this horrid spectacle winds its shrieking way through the city – spectators who, by their moans and tears, only add horror to the scene. At times the sight is too much for one or two, who suddenly start cutting at themselves with pocket-knives or any sharp instrument they can get hold of, and have to be restrained by force. Relatives of each head-cutter accompany the procession and, the moment one drops unconscious from loss of blood, pick him up and carry him to the nearest 'hammam' or bath, while another carries a new outfit of clothes. In the bath, his wounds are washed and covered with what I believe to be bitumen. He slowly recovers. By three o'clock in the afternoon he is completely restored, and can be seen galloping to and fro on horseback, taking part in the famous Passion Play, which is the representation of the Battle of Kerbela. This latter spectacle ends the day, and completes the more important ceremonies. It is a very respectable performance after all that has gone before, but in some parts is intensely realistic. The audience behave as though the real battle were being enacted before them. He who takes the part of Yazid must be a man of iron nerve, so threatening is the audience. Small Arab children are enlisted as supers. They represent the children of Hussein and his followers. A horseman, dressed in marvellous armour of a special colour, gallops towards them bearing an earthenware mug of water, which he gives to them, and gallops away. At once from the other side rides out a warrior, who knocks the mug out of their hands with his spear, just as they are about to drink. The children cry, 'Atshan, atshan!' (thirsty, thirsty), and members of the audience weep bitterly at the memory of the pangs of thirst which brought about the downfall of the gallant little band under the leadership of Hussein.

On one occasion I was invited by the Killidar (Treasurer) of the Shrine at Najaf to be present in the Sahan to witness the arrival of the band of Syeds, the Servants of the Shrine referred to above. It was about 10.30 p.m. on the night before the tenth. The Sahan is the building adjoining the mosque in which the treasure is said to be stored.

We sat waiting for them in the courtyard, without light of any kind. The house rose up dimly in the darkness all round us. Above could be seen a few stars on a cloudless, moonless sky; and high up on the balconies surrounding the yard we could just distinguish the huddled-up forms of some women of the household. We sat in absolute silence on a raised covered-in dais at one end. Now and

MUHARRAM

again would be heard the dull thuds from a party of breast-beaters in some part of the city. A man comes in to tell us that they are on the way, and fades away into the darkness. A few minutes later we hear the approach of a large crowd, that curious, silent approach characteristic of a large body of men actuated by some deep religious motive. Lights begin to flicker on the wall, reflections from the torches without. Gradually the courtyard fills. There are four torches, immense braziers on the ends of long poles, and round each brazier a dim group of Syeds. Many of them were personally known to me, and others I knew by reputation. They were of all ages, some mere boys of twelve years, others bearded and bowed men well past sixty. The only mark distinguishing them as descendants of the Prophet was the small green turban that each was still wearing. All were stripped to the waist. Suddenly a young child, not more than thirteen years old, stood up on the dais. At a sign from the Killidar I also stood up, keeping well in the background. The child began to read the story of the Passion of Hussein.

I have always thought that Arabic was a most musical language, and this child had been chosen for the beauty of his reading. He showed little emotion, reading the simple facts in his childish treble, clearly and slowly. At each pause came the dull blow – a curious effect of restrained intensity. In the smoky glow of those torches I saw hundreds of arms flinging themselves up to heaven, I saw those two hundred and fifty men and boys, the majority of them so hypocritically respectable in their everyday life, now stripped to the skin, fervently striking their breasts in honour of their martyrs, while from above could be heard the passionate grieving of the women.

Here was no wildness, no lack of control. And I felt, and still feel, that at that moment I had touched upon all that is good and vital in Islam, that potential devotion and religious fervour which, directed along right channels, would move the world.

We have here a people who not only have a natural genius for religion, but are at the same time aching to express themselves, while hampered by a system of faith that hems them in with restrictions and limitations. It is not surprising that at such times as Muharram we find them letting themselves go in a way which to the superficial observer is only extravagant and ludicrous. The pathos of it is profoundly moving.

And even in Muharram it is the people themselves who have forced this concession from their religious leaders. These extreme exhibitions of grief and mortification are absolutely 'haram' (forbidden). It was the Chief Mujtahid himself who, in a confidential moment, confessed to me with regret that in this matter he could not control his people. It would be easier to hold back the waves of the sea than to curb so fundamental a primitive emotion of the human race as its devotion to God; for this is the underlying principle of all the Muharram ceremonies, though none of the participants have the least idea of the fact.

I asked one of the head-cutters why he did it. He laughed and said he didn't know. As he was a person of rather greater intelligence than the aver-

MUHARRAM

age, I pressed him for a reason, and he finally said he thought that 'everything was better' as the result. He could not make himself any clearer; but he explained to me that, though by acting in this way he thought there was a good chance of his own shortcomings being overlooked, he could not be sure of forgiveness. Still it certainly pleased God and 'everything was better'.

This certainly bears a close resemblance to the Law of Mystical Substitution; and there is not, I think, any doubt that the vast majority of the human race does actually attach great value to suffering voluntarily endured, not merely as discipline to the individual sufferer, but because of a vague consciousness that as a result 'everything is better'. Arabs, especially among the children, have a truer knowledge of real religion than hundreds of pious Anglo-Saxons who attend their Sunday service and peruse the *Church Times* on Friday mornings. For every Arab knows that religion means a certain amount of discomfort which the great majority do cheerfully undergo. But, as I have said, they are a people with a natural genius for religion.

They are a childlike, primitive, and uneducated folk to whom Allah is ever present in their lives, far more so than in our own. He is a God to be feared and to be prayed to from afar; but their prayers are full of praise and little else. That this praise is offered more often than not in the spirit of propitiation is I think certain. His Name occurs in almost every sentence – in the ordinary etiquette of greeting, after bathing, after washing, in short in most of the activities of daily life. The

THE INS AND OUTS OF MESOPOTAMIA

Name is ever before man in his waking consciousness, and yet, who can love this God? Therefore, the universal desire of love towards Him who, as revealed by their very faith, is unlovable, must be appeased by extravagantly expressed devotion to those whom they believe to be His Saints. It is only in times like Muharram and Ramadhan that we can catch glimpses of the real fundamentals of the Arab character and of its sterling worth.

CHAPTER IV

FASTING AND RAMADHAN

Effects on work. A *genuine* fast. Comparison with Christian 'practice'. The great feast.

TO THE EUROPEAN who has lived in the East, the Fast of Ramadhan is the most familiar of all Muslim ordinances, for it is the one that affects him most. His servants and his office personnel become more and more languid as the month progresses, increasingly haggard and unconscionably touchy.

Fasting is the third of the duties of obligation in Islam. The Quranic authority is found in Sura ii. 183 and onwards, which I give in full.

183. O you who believe! fasting is prescribed for you, as it was prescribed for those before you,[1] so that you may guard against evil,

184. for a certain number of days; but whoever among you is sick or on a journey, then he shall fast a like number of other days; and those who are able to do it may effect a redemption by feeding a poor man; so whoever does

---

[1] Christians and Jews.

THE INS AND OUTS OF MESOPOTAMIA

good spontaneously it is better for him; and that you fast is better for you if you know.

185. The month of Ramadhan is that in which the Quran was revealed, a guidance to men and clear proofs of the guidance and the distinction;[1] therefore whoever of you is present in the month he shall fast therein, and whoever is sick or upon a journey, then he shall fast a like number of other days; Allah desires ease for you and He does not desire for you difficulty, and He desires that you should complete the number and that you should exalt the greatness of Allah for His having guided you, and that you may give thanks.

187. It is made lawful for you to go in to your wives on the night of the fast; they are an apparel for you and you are an apparel for them; Allah knew that you acted unfaithfully to yourselves,[2] so He has turned to you mercifully and removed from you this burden; so now be in contact with them and seek what Allah has ordained for you, and eat and drink until the whiteness of the day becomes distinct from the blackness of the night at dawn, and then complete the fast till night, and have not contact with them while you keep to the mosques;[3] these are the limits of Allah, so do not go near them. Thus does Allah make clear His communications for men that they may guard against evil.

The Fast of Ramadhan is of the very greatest importance, and a right understanding of its significance is most necessary in the rapid survey that we have undertaken. In spite of the plain words of verse 187, there are restrictions which

1 I.e. between good and evil.
2 I.e. by abstaining from conjugal intercourse.
3 This refers to those who pass day and night in the mosques during the last ten days of the month.

FASTING AND RAMADHAN

every Shia' observes, contrary to the instructions laid down there. The fast is of course 'of obligation' on all Muslims, with the exception of young children under the age of puberty, sick persons, the aged, and those travelling. But in the case of the sick and travellers, they must keep the fast afterwards. The number of days must be made up, so that every Muslim will have kept one month of strict fast every year. This fast differs entirely from the conception of a fast as held by the Catholic Church. The strict Christian fast, which is of obligation on every Christian unless a dispensation has been received from his Bishop, permits the taking of eight ounces of food in the morning, one full meal about 3 p.m., and four ounces at night. Meat is of course entirely excluded; and in the lesser meals butter and fats are also prohibited. The only occasion when this endures for any length of time is during the forty days of Lent, but the rigour of the fast is enormously alleviated by the counting of each Sunday as a feast-day. It is significant of the lack of discipline in the Anglican Church that Bishops rarely consider it necessary to give a dispensation, and that the fast in Lent, as distinct from abstinence, is almost universally disregarded throughout Western Christendom.

The Fast of Ramadhan, however, is a complete fast from sunrise to sunset for the period of one lunar month. In modern Islam the extent to which this is carried is almost absurd, the majority of the people suffering from what Catholic theologians would call 'scrupulous conscience'. Neither food nor drink of any kind may pass the lips. Even if a little water should be accidentally swallowed when washing the teeth, the fast is broken. No medicine may be taken, even though it be put into the ear or nose, and enemata of any kind are equally forbidden. Neither are accidents condoned, for should a small piece of food lodge in the interstices of the teeth and be swallowed during the day, the fast is broken, as it is if anyone takes food under a misapprehension as to the time. Many consider that a swallowing of the saliva breaks the fast. Moreover, all smoking is absolutely forbidden – a most serious deprivation; and equally, of course, all taking of drugs. Perfume must not be used, and certainly among the Shia', cohabitation is rigorously avoided during the whole month.

It is frequently stated by Europeans who have spent some time in the East that the fast is, comparatively speaking, mere parade, because the people are permitted to eat as they like during the night. Such a prejudiced and ignorant charge could not be made by anyone who took the least trouble to try to understand and sympathise with the people among whom he lives; and we have a very different account of the matter from the greatest of all authorities upon Arabia and the Arabs – Sir Richard Burton.

Those who accuse the Muslim of hypocrisy, indeed, do not profess to know the facts; but are content to say that, *if so severe a fast were strictly observed*, it would be bound to have a far more obvious effect upon the physique of the 'faithful'.

It is not inaccurate, I think, to say that many who live in wealth and luxury have lost all sense of their religious obligations, as they have in every faith:

FASTING AND RAMADHAN

'How hard it is for a rich man to enter into the Kingdom of Heaven.'

As Professor Margoliouth has written: 'The poor in Egypt or Syria are the scrupulous worshippers who fast throughout Ramadhan . . . Comfort brings indifference.' And this is generally true of both India and Mesopotamia, though in the latter country the Sheikhs of the tribes are as strict as their 'fellaliyeh'.

Neither is it true that the people eat so much during the night that it is easy for them to last out during the day.

Owing to the Muslim year being composed of lunar months, the conditions of life during the fast vary annually. During the past few years it has occurred in the height of the hot weather; so that, if there were free indulgence during the night, it would have brought scarcely any relief.

Would these critics be prepared to carry on their ordinary work for fifteen or sixteen hours (during eight of which the temperature was anything from 116 to 125 degrees in the shade or even higher), without a drop of liquid refreshment?

But, to my mind, it is even more astonishing that these people do give up smoking entirely. Tobacco, in the form of 'huqqahs' and cigarettes, plays a very large part in their lives; and yet at the sound of the gun announcing the commencement of the fast, it is laid aside without a murmur of complaint.

I have dwelt on this point because I believe the supercilious and superior attitude of Englishmen abroad has done immense harm to the Empire. We all know the old gentleman who returns, after per-

THE INS AND OUTS OF MESOPOTAMIA

haps twenty years' service in India, and lays down the law on all things Indian to a circle of admiring stay-at-home relatives and friends on the ground that he 'knows India'!

I well remember the shame I felt, during the war, to find that I could not understand a word of what a Yorkshire miner in my squad was saying to me. Yet I suppose I might be allowed to say that I 'know England'! The fact of the matter is that most of us have a fairly exhaustive knowledge of our own little cabbage-patch. But when it comes to claiming a 'knowledge' of a continent, crammed full of different races, different tongues, different colours, and different forms of worship, and above all of different mentalities, it is a different matter. Too many of us are content with 'knowledge' obtained through the medium of Government offices or of commercial undertakings, and the educative value of such 'knowledge' speaks for itself. I cannot help thinking that the cruel and unjust criticism so frequently made of the fasting Muslim is perhaps largely due to the emotion of hurt pride. Such critics know very well that, whereas they themselves do not keep the mild rules of abstinence enjoined by their own faith, they hate the silent reproach of so severe a mortification, undertaken in obedience to a faith of which they know nothing and for which they care less.

The fast is broken at sunset, usually by a cup of tea. It is a sight full of interest to see the coffee-shops filling up about 7 p.m. The 'nirghilehs' are brought out and placed before the somewhat worn and haggard-looking clients, who sit chatting with each other on ordinary topics, betraying neither

FASTING AND RAMADHAN

discontent nor dissatisfaction. To do so would be highly improper. Any sign of a desire for the swift passage of those last few minutes is sternly repressed – and how slowly they must seem to pass!

At last the sunset gun is heard, or in smaller places the cry of the Mueddhin. The cups of tea are hastily brought round, but the attendants are limited; and now one sees the true dignity of the Arab. Someone must come last, but there is no shouting, no show of impatience, no expressed desire to be served before their neighbour. A muttered 'Al hamdu lillah'[1] may perhaps greet the report of the gun, and that is all. The longed-for 'istekhan' (glass cup) is deliberately held in the hand a moment before drinking, lest any undue impatience be shown. With a quiet 'Bismillah!'[2] it is at last slowly sipped, and the first cigarette or 'nirghile' of the day set going.

It should be remarked, too, that such strict observance is not ever considered worthy to excite remark. It is 'of obligation', a duty, and that is all. Those who fail to keep the fast, on the other hand, are subjected to most unfavourable comment, and indeed often addressed by the insulting term of 'kafir' (unbeliever) or Nasrani (Christian).

In Government offices the hours are altered, so far as possible, to allow as much rest through the hottest part of the day as is commensurate with efficiency. But in the summer, this cannot be much extended beyond the normal afternoon siesta. During this month, however, special permission is given to the coffee-shops to keep open during the

[1] Praise be to God!
[2] In the name of God.

THE INS AND OUTS OF MESOPOTAMIA

night; and a few reckless spirits literally turn night into day, but they are very generally despised.

The discipline for the night consists of two meals: the 'iftar', or that which formally breaks the fast, taken after sunset, and the 'sakhari', or the meal before sunrise. In Mesopotamia the times for these are about 8.30 p.m. and 2.30 a.m. Special devotions also have to be added to the usual prayers. Greater time and more care are taken over them, and in the mosque at night it is the custom to say twenty 'rakats'. These are read from the Quran by an Imam, each 'rakat' containing a few verses, and being terminated by a prostration. This practice is carried out mostly in the Sunni mosques, as I can testify from an unfortunate personal experience in Baghdad. The Imam in a particular mosque, not more than twenty yards from my house, was singularly competent in the 'Ilmu't-Tajwid, or science of chanting the Quran, and every night during Ramadhan he would give a public exhibition of his ability from the minaret of the mosque. I found my rest considerably curtailed, as the pious individual persisted in chanting at the top of his voice with quite incredible vigour for well over an hour every night!

It is inevitable that such real and continued physical self-denial should cause general irritation, which increases as the time draws to an end. It is well known that those responsible for law and order must expect special anxieties during the month. All sorts of causes will contribute to sudden outbursts of ill-feeling against the 'kafir', which may take many different forms. The ner-

FASTING AND RAMADHAN

vous strain must be tremendous; and a certain amount of disturbance is practically inevitable.

Yet I can say from my own personal knowledge that, so far as Baghdad is concerned, there is no increase of petty crime during that month – if anything, rather the reverse.

The bad feeling is always directed against the non-Muslim, and it arises, I think, from a conscious superiority to the unbeliever, felt by those in the subordinate position of a governed race. I have never heard it expressed in so many words, though I have frequently been questioned as to the rules of fasting observed by Christians! The Muslim knows perfectly well that there are such rules, and that they ought to be observed. He must draw one of two conclusions:

(1) If the Christian faith is worth anything at all, then the Christians who do not observe the less comfortable obligations of that faith are worthless men. Or

(2) As many Christians who do not seem worthless, but are, on the contrary, quite pleasant and honest individuals, do *not* observe these regulations, it must be because in their hearts they know that their faith is false.

The devout Shia' cannot understand compromise in this matter. No explanation or excuse as to health, or living in an unsuitable climate, will satisfy him. He knows perfectly well that however ill he himself may feel during Ramadhan he will not break his fast; and he is driven to the logical conclusion that in this particular matter he is a better man. Can we say that his reasoning is entirely without foundation?

THE INS AND OUTS OF MESOPOTAMIA

Once this idea enters his mind, the nightly sermons in the mosques offer a great opportunity for its cultivation and fruition. He is now, naturally, nervous, irritable, and ready for any quarrel. His race has, for the time, become a brotherhood of common discomfort, and indeed suffering: the 'kafir' Government, and the individuals thereof, must be common objects of dislike. Hence the strained atmosphere which is always present during the month of Ramadhan.

I cannot close this chapter without mentioning the conclusion of the fast – the 'Id al Fitr, or Great Feast, which ushers in the beginning of the ensuing month. I believe that I am correct in saying that this feast has no Quranic authority. It comes from mere spontaneous exuberance of spirits, to a people, ordinarily self-indulgent to the last degree, who find themselves suddenly released from a self-imposed discipline and mortification of no light nature. I have seen the keeping of this feast in the desert, in towns, and on board ship, and have always wished that I too had kept the fast!

On the 28th or 29th of the month – I speak of the scene in a riverain village – the people will gather together towards sunset. Try as they will, they cannot conceal their anxiety. They are restless, strolling about from group to group, and casting anxious looks towards that quarter of the sky where the moon may be expected to appear. Watchers are posted on the highest roofs. I happened to be a witness of much confusion in a certain village one year, owing to the action of the Imam of the Mosque. He was a very old man and excessively proud of having retained, *as he*

FASTING AND RAMADHAN

believed, his full powers of sight and hearing, although he was, in fact, as deaf as a post and more than half blind. His position, of course, would — under ordinary circumstances — have given him an authority none dare dispute; and when the village folk simply refused to believe his assertion that the moon had NOT risen, his fury was incredibly comic. He finally went home in a huff, presumably to keep the fast until full-moon, for it was quite certain that he would never see anything smaller!

As the minutes pass, a strained silence steals over all. Suddenly a shout is heard — the new moon has risen. Is it true? Perhaps it is only a mistake — or, as one might say, a suppressed desire. The crowd rush helter-skelter to some point of vantage, old men and young boys jostling each other in confusion. It is the law that each must see for himself. Perhaps it is a cloudy evening, and when they have arrived the moon is no longer visible. The awful intensity of their expressions as they wait for its reappearance must be seen to be appreciated. At last it appears — an almost invisible crescent. The ensuing scene beggars description. Head over heels they tumble down from the roofs of the houses. Shouts of 'Al hamdu lillah![1] Allahu akbar!' mingle with the unrestrained laughter of exuberant joy. Some — the more devout — perhaps have begun a prayer, regardless of the hubbub around. Others are rushing about, distributing kisses broadcast. Anyone who has a rifle will let it off as rapidly as he can, to the imminent danger of his neighbours, whereby hangs a tale.

[1] Praise be to God. God is great.

THE INS AND OUTS OF MESOPOTAMIA

A certain Political Officer had been much worried over the theft of a British rifle and ammunition from those supplied to the Arab 'shebanah' or levies. In the midst of the confusion and hubbub of greetings to the new moon, clear and distinct from the heavy detonation of the Arab rifle, sounded the sharp 'ping' of a .303, and it came from the palm gardens across the river. Taking two Arabs with him, he at once crossed, and met the culprit, hastening towards the scene of general rejoicing, letting off Government ammunition as hard as he could. When arrested, the offender at first had not the slightest idea of his offence, until reiterated explanations at last penetrated a brain drunk with joy, and he awoke to the fact that a 'stolen rifle' was in his hand! Truly 'in the midst of life', etc.; but this well shows the devil-may-care spirit of the 'Id al Fitr. In this particular case the rigour of the law was not enforced, I am glad to say!

It is on the following day that the Oriental love of colour runs amok. Every servant has extracted from his master, by fair means or by foul, the wherewithal for the purchase of new clothes. During the last few days of Ramadhan the dyer reaps a rich harvest, and to the European eye the combinations are distracting. To the Government official it is a fatiguing day. He must entertain in his office all the Government servants, coffee and sweets are handed round, and to every man he gives the greeting "Idkum mubarak!"[1] He must then embark on a round of complimentary calls on

1 May your feast be blessed!

FASTING AND RAMADHAN

all the important people, particularly those of the Religious Hierarchy, and in the course of his visits is driven to consume incredible quantities of coffee, tea, sherbet, and sweetmeats, one after another. In the evening his house is filled with those who come to call upon him, for their own *joie de vivre* must, so far as possible, be shared; and they delight to include their friend, even though, through no fault of his own, he be a 'kafir'.

On this day they are all just lovable children, and some of my happiest memories are of the 'Id al Fitr.

If Muharram shows the Shia' at the height of religious emotion, Ramadhan exhibits their capacity for using the will in connection with personal discipline. The fact that it is the rule of their faith makes it none the less remarkable, and it is a standing example of what the will can accomplish.

As a race, the Anglo-Saxon, in his private life, is infinitely more disciplined than the Oriental. The exercise of the will is an ever-present necessity in his daily experience if he wishes to succeed. The rush of competition compels this. Not so with the Arab. If ever there was a person who conducted his affairs on the principle of *laissez-faire*, it is he. Every proposal put forward, every order given, is met by 'Inshallah' or 'Inshallah bukra';[1] or, in other words, 'At all costs put off what can be done tomorrow.' Their sexual morality is quite incredibly lax, while, in the privacy of their homes, opium, hashish, and to a lesser extent alcohol, play a very large part. The only thing in which

---

1 If God wills, or, Tomorrow if God wills!

THE INS AND OUTS OF MESOPOTAMIA

they can be said to take a real interest, if effort be any index to interest, is the accumulation of money.

Yet, at a moment's notice they will suddenly exert the sternest self-control over their utterly uncontrolled natures, voluntarily undergoing a discipline which would do credit to the professed of some religious order, and which, if practised by a Christian layman for the sake of his faith, would gain for him an enduring reputation for sanctity, or perhaps, in these days, for insanity.

However, despite the sneers of the modern world, it was of such stuff that the first converts to Christianity were made, and it is not difficult to account for the spread of the early Church. Neither is it difficult to see the danger of Islam spreading at the expense of Christianity, when its laity are prepared to undergo personal discipline and discomfort of so severe a degree for the sake of their belief. The strict observance of Ramadhan is due to the fact that it is laid down in the Quran in so many words, and that the Quran is the actual word of God Himself. In the New Testament there is also a definite order to fast.

It is well known that the 'Believers' have *no respect* for a convert to Islam; a man who leaves his own faith, they hold, is not to be trusted, in this world or the next. But one who neglects his own faith, while he nominally lives by it, is even more to be despised.

CHAPTER V

SHIA' AND SUNNI

Shia' doctrine, the Saints. Need for a 'spiritual' or supernatural (i.e. divinely appointed) leader, to preserve unity. Unique position of Ali. The people did *not* want Feisal. Narrowness and isolation of the Shia'.

THE NORMAL PROGRESS OF peoples in the world has been marked by definite stages.

We have first the nomad tribes living from hand to mouth, only bound together by the ties of consanguinity, and existing by robbery of their neighbours and the slaughter of animals. The next stage is marked by a reversal of the last characteristic. Instead of animals being valued for destruction, their preservation came to be the important factor, and the tribal interest gradually turned from robbery to the protection of herds and flocks, with all the natural mental development that such protection would imply. From this stage arises the desire in the individual for a settlement of some kind, and the pastoral community turns its attention to cultivation. From this stage again to that of the town dweller is but a step.

We have in Iraq these four stages existing almost side by side. The majority of the inhabitants

THE INS AND OUTS OF MESOPOTAMIA

are cultivators; but, as has been pointed out, the impetus in mental and social activity comes from the towns in general, and from the Holy Cities in particular; but the degree of development which we might normally expect is singularly lacking. The great characteristic of the tribal state of Society is the unity that exists within the tribe, and more especially in the families that compose that tribe. This, as I shall shortly show, is conspicuous by its absence, so that the majority of the Iraqis are even below the normal of their elementary condition. It is, I believe, their system of theology which keeps them back; and, though a complete unravelling of Shia' theology would take many volumes, I propose to touch upon those differences which render it distinct from that of the Sunni, in support of this opinion.

The profession of faith, common to all Islam, has with the Shia' a most important addition.

'La illah illa Allah wa Muhammad rasul Allah' is the Islamic creed. The Shia' adds, 'Wa Ali Wali Allah.' 'There is no god but THE God, and Muhammad is the apostle of God, *and Ali is the Saint of God.*'

This addition is emphasised particularly during the ceremonies of Muharram. Each band of devotees, as they shuffle along from place to place, in paces of only a few inches, all chant in an excited, quick monotone:

'Maku Wali illa Ali!' ('There is no saint but Ali!')

Each word coincides with the fall of the foot. This constant reiteration is, of course, taken up by the bystanders, and the rhyming rhythm of the

SHIA' AND SUNNI

short phrase necessarily acts as a most powerful excitant on the lines of auto-suggestion.

It is worth our while to notice, in passing, how frequently this form of rhymed prose occurs in Arabic. It is considered highly attractive even in ordinary speech. The Quran is very largely rhymed, thereby producing the musical lilt so dear to the heart of the Arab. The first few verses of the Fatiha, the first chapter, will suffice as an example:

Bismillah al rahman al rahim,	In the Name of God, the Beneficent, the Merciful,
Al hamdu lillah, rab al alamin,	Praise is due to Allah the Lord of the Worlds,
Malak yaum al din,	Master of the Day of Requital,
Al rahman al rahim.	The Beneficent, the Merciful.

It may be thought that I am emphasising unimportant detail, but when the exceedingly low standard of mentality possessed by the Arab in general is realised, and the ease with which such rhythmic rhyming sentences can be remembered, their value will be appreciated. One cannot help wishing that Christian Missions to Muslim countries could employ this simple device, and translate some of our Christian formulae in the same way. The Pater Noster, Ave, Gloria, and Credo could all, with a little effort and great advantage, be rendered in the same style. It may be remembered that the Gnostics used this method.

I once mentioned the idea to a missionary in Palestine, but he was horrified at the mere idea that anything so holy as the Christian profession of faith could in any way resemble so wicked a book as the Quran!

The last phrase in the profession of faith – 'Wa Ali Wali Allah' – leads us on to the cornerstone of Shia' doctrine – the Imamate, which is entirely distinct from the Sunni doctrine of the Khaliphate.

This doctrine arose from the instinctive desire in the heart of the early Muslims for a Spiritual Head, as distinct from a Religious Head: a distinction that perhaps needs some explanation, which a passing glance at the conditions under which the pre-Islamite Arabs lived may provide. They were – and are – a quarrelsome, quick-tempered people. Intertribal and interfamily feuds were the order of the day, and these feuds were kept alive for countless generations. To carry on the ancient enmity was part of the family honour, and the recounting of the old fights, feats, and victories formed the staple subject of social intercourse. A more disunited people it would be hard to find, till, suddenly, the miracle took place! A man arose who, by his personality and *by his claim to direct divine guidance*, actually brought about the impossible – namely, the union of all these warring factions.

The Arabs are a grossly superstitious people, and at the same time self-indulgent and licentious. By a supremely brilliant combination of these two elements in his teaching, Muhammad produced a hitherto unheard-of result.

The immediate effect was that the power of the newly-formed Arab nation, previously composed of quarrelsome and contentious communities, became almost invincible. The advantage of unity was apparent to all. A people who had for years lived by

SHIA' AND SUNNI

raiding and loot were quick to appreciate the vast profit that accrued to them in the new warfare, a profit formerly unheard of. This naturally included the women-folk of the conquered nations, and the rapid increase of the feminine element compelled the authoritative introduction of polygamy. Apart altogether from these more material benefits which the administration of Muhammad had brought about, the personal appeal he made to each of his followers was tremendous. It chiefly lay in his claim to have personal communication with God, through the angel Gabriel. To appreciate this it must be realised what a tremendous influence the unseen exercises on the Arab of the present day. It is undoubtedly the result of their dwelling in the great open spaces of the world, their familiarity with the mysterious fascination of the desert. No doubt Muhammad himself felt this influence, and he established the belief in angels and the Ginn as an essential part of the faith of every Muslim.

On the death of the Prophet – this great personality who had held all these warring elements together – the old divisions and rivalries very soon began to reappear. The election of Abu Bakr as the Khaliph of Islam did little to preserve unity. He and his successors could not hold the people together. There was no supernatural appeal in their leadership, nothing which definitely placed them above the common ruck of mankind, save their material circumstances. What was wanted was one to stand out above all, the undoubted and universally recognised Leader, who would be looked up to as such by all the different factions. Such a leader

THE INS AND OUTS OF MESOPOTAMIA

was ultimately found in the person of the Imam. It seemed impossible that a people who for so long had been singled out by God for the honour of the one and only perfect Revelation vouchsafed to humanity, communicated by a Heavenly Messenger to one of themselves, should now be left without anything more than an ordinary man to direct them. More and more, the existence of political factions and mutual jealousy emphasised the necessity for a *divinely* appointed Head, and this desire became definitely crystallised in the circumstances surrounding the murders of Ali and Hasan, and the death of Hussein on the Plain of Kerbela.

It is obvious that if the Head of Islam were under divine guidance he must be a member of the family of the Prophet. The personal reputation of Ali, his bravery in warfare, his devotion to the Prophet, above all his relationship to the Prophet (he was his son-in-law and cousin), all pointed to him as the one chosen – the Imam, the Exemplar, the Mediator; to be succeeded by Imams equally divine.

The growth of this doctrine was remarkable. To trace it step by step would be impracticable, but the Imam as he is today, in the eyes of the Shia', will show its development. He is sinless, even the taint of original sin being warded off. His physical body is declared to be different from that of the ordinary man, infinitely more delicate and casting no shadow. He is greater than all the prophets, and his special function is that of mediator between the people and God.

SHIA' AND SUNNI

Professor Browne, in *The Episode of the Bab*, writes:

'The Imam of the Shia's is the divinely ordained successor of the Prophet, endowed with all perfections and spiritual gifts, one whom all the faithful must obey, whose decision is absolute and final, whose wisdom is superhuman and whose words are authoritative.'

The Rev. Edward Sell adds:

'The Imam is the supreme Pontiff, the Vicar of God upon earth.'

These superhuman, and almost divine, qualities have become part of the Imam's nature through the doctrine of 'nur' or the 'light'. I enquired about this 'light' from some of the Ulema, and so far as I could understand it, the 'light' is the essence of the nature of God. It is His Being and has existed from all eternity. This 'light' existed in itself, and it was not until the birth of Muhammad that God gave out a ray from this eternal source which attached itself to the Prophet. It then appeared in the world for the first time. This 'ray' is continued by right of office to each Imam, beginning with Ali, and being itself divine, confers what can only be described as a part of divinity on the possessor of it.

It would be thought that each of the Imams, of whom there have been twelve,[1] would be equal in

---

[1] Though the last (twelfth) Imam disappeared, as a boy of twelve, his 'death' has never been proved or admitted. He is still 'expected', the Mahdi (hence, without a suc-

glory, and the orthodox Shia' would formally affirm this. But the circumstances surrounding the deaths of Ali, Hasan, and Hussein, and the family relationship between the former and the Prophet, has exalted Ali into a unique position. It is largely from the desire to exalt Ali that the doctrine of the Imamate has been so far developed. One cannot be surprised that almost divine honour is given to him; and there are some who definitely consider that Ali was divine, was the incarnation of God.

It is easy to see how far the Shia' has travelled from the position held by the Sunni. The latter hold the doctrine of the Khaliphate (i.e. a human Pontiff), and absolutely deny the very idea of the Imamate. They are therefore considered by the Shia' as heretics and accursed. The Shia' care nothing for the political question of the Khaliphate that has been agitating the Middle East for so long. The only interest that they might have in it is a desire to see the hated Sunni suppressed.

This feeling is naturally strongest in the Holy Cities. The parallelism between Muharram and Good Friday is now seen to be far closer than might originally have been thought; it celebrates the martyrdom of the Mediator.

The Sunni is regarded by the Shia' in the same way as the Jew was regarded by the medieval Christian. He is beyond the pale, doomed to Hell, and far worse than the Jew or Christian. The

---

cessor), and it is the various 'pretender' Imams who have from time to time thrown Islam into religious ferment and internecine wars.

SHIA' AND SUNNI

hatred between the two is well shown in the following incident, which occurred during Ramadhan of 1920. Two devout Shia', with a broader outlook on life than is usual, left Kerbela on a visit to Baghdad. The feeling against the British Administration was very acute at the time, and these two thought it an excellent opportunity to try and effect a union between the Sunni and Shia', or, as they called it, a 'tauhid'. Accordingly they fraternised with the 'heretics' as much as possible and were well received. When they attended the Sunni mosques, the people kissed their hands, and all seemed to be going well. It must have been a most inspiring sight! But unfortunately some evilly disposed person saw this going on and took the news to the Chief Mujtahid, Mirza Muhammad Taqi Shirazi, who was in residence at Kerbela, and quickly summoned the two pious souls to his holy presence. They accordingly returned to Kerbela, fully expecting to be warmly congratulated on their holy work. They entered the presence and were courteously received by the great man, who was surrounded by the customary attendants. He asked them in a kindly voice about the work they had been doing in Baghdad, and, anxious to exalt themselves, they even went beyond the strict truth. When they were thus convicted many times over out of their own mouths, before many witnesses, the attitude of the Holy Man completely changed, and they began to wish they had not been quite so enthusiastic. Having addressed them at some length, he ended his discourse something as follows: 'Not only have you true Muslims had dealings with those sons of dogs, the Sunnis; but you have actually entered their mosques. Further, coming from the Holy City of Kerbela and being known to have so come, you have brought disgrace on the Shrines of Holy Abbas and Hussein. In addition to penance subsequently to be inflicted, you will receive three hundred lashes apiece.'

These were duly administered, and the two, very sore and very angry, went and complained to the Political Officer, who was a Persian, and from whom I heard the whole story!

It is largely this question of religious antagonism that makes the Turks so intensely hated in Iraq. For the Jews and the Christians have not had the opportunity of becoming believers, whereas the Sunni has had every opportunity and is therefore a renegade.

When, therefore, the Colonial Office was induced to put Feisal, son of the Shariff of Sunni Mecca, on the throne of Shia' Iraq, it can be understood that it was *utterly against the people's wish*.

The intense feeling between the two is hardly realised in Baghdad, for Baghdad is the centre of the ex-Turkish official, of whom the great majority are naturally Sunni. Speaking generally – of course there are exceptions – a more corrupt class could hardly be imagined. Owing to the dearth of trained men, the British Administration were compelled to utilise some of these 'effendis' at the beginning. One of the Ulema of Kerbela made the following trite remark to Sir A. T. Wilson, the Civil Commissioner: 'When a man pulls down a public latrine because it smells too bad, it is a mistake to build the new one with the same bricks!'

SHIA' AND SUNNI

I have dealt with this question at some length, because it appears to me not only grossly unfair to the people themselves, but equally so to the people at home, who have to pay for a policy which is described, without the slightest justification, as 'giving the people of the country the Government that they desire'. This is utterly untrue. It is a truism, I regret to say, that the name of the British is 'mud' throughout the Middle East; it is ludicrous to pretend that our present policy has been pursued from motives of 'philanthropy'! It was a sorry day for us when Whitehall was compelled to back the house of the Shariff of Mecca, which only increased the feeling against us.

It might be supposed that the doctrine of the Imamate, with the Mujtahid's right to freely interpret the Law, would give more elasticity to the Shia' faith, and thus open the way to greater progress than the rigidity of the Sunni system would permit. But this has not proved to be the case. The doctrine of the Imamate has cut them off even from their own kind, for the Shia' is in the minority in Islam. It is a truism that progress is only to be attained by contact with other nations and by a constant infusion of new thought into the community-consciousness. The Shia' in particular, and Islam in general, are cut off from the world. They have built themselves in with impassable walls of prejudice and bigotry. 'The more self-centred and exclusive any people, starting from the basis of very special conditions, can make its life, the further will its condition be from corresponding to the ideal of human society . . . There is in it no germ of progress; its morality, which has only

THE INS AND OUTS OF MESOPOTAMIA

grown up through custom, has not the flexibility which can only be given by general principles; it presses upon individuals with the force of rigid prejudice, and condemns all those individual impulses running counter to the narrow-mindedness of tradition, which now and then arise from the inextinguishable diversities of human nature. Hence all such civilisations ... are characterised by unintelligent intolerance, and this only disappears when, having been forced into contact with the morality of other nations, men's illusion as to the universal validity of their own maxims is destroyed, and they are constrained to learn in their most comprehensive form those universal moral obligations without the recognition of which no human society can exist.'[1] This might have been written of the Shia' community of Iraq. Cursed, as the country is, with the presence of the Holy Cities, it is foredoomed to stagnation unless there comes a speedy reform, either from without or from within.

The former would imply a civil administration of such power that the strength of the Mujtahidun could be shattered. Under present conditions, any proposal of which the Hierarchy disapproves is said to 'dakhil fi'l diyana' – that is, it 'enters into religion'. In other words, it interferes with their particular prerogative. It is easy to see, with their ability to split hairs, and their power of interpretation, how anything and everything can be said to 'interfere with religious matters'. A reform from within would imply a change of faith. It is my

1 Lotze's *Microcosmus*, vol. ii. p. 499.

SHIA' AND SUNNI

belief that, given the right kind of men and a right system, the introduction of Christianity would not prove so hopeless a task as has been generally assumed. There are certain aspects of the Doctrine of the Imamate which are not unfavourable. The mediatory conception of the Imam is, undoubtedly, an example of the wish being father to the thought. It is very striking that, through the martyrdom of Hussein, the essentially Christian idea of a 'suffering Mediator', if not combined in one person, is united in the one family. The impulsive, emotional nature of the Arab of Iraq, under the impetus of Persia, required something more satisfying than the unapproachable Deity offered him by the Prophet. During Muharram, Hussein and Ali are inextricably interwoven. The ignorance of the ordinary people is almost incredible. I have met Najafis who thought that Ali and Hussein were two names for one person! The significance is at once obvious.

It is, no doubt, the voice of the people that directs theological development to a very large extent. We have had a similar example in England during the past few years.

The duty of the faithful to offer prayers for the departed is clearly laid down by the Catholic Church, and has been universally practised throughout those communions which owe obedience to Rome and to the Patriarch of the Eastern Church. Only the Church of England held aloof from this practice. When a few conscientious priests encouraged their people to pray for the dead, they were practically accused of crime, and – in some cases – suffered a considerable amount of persecution. But now there are comparatively few churches in which the faithful departed are not remembered. This change is in no way due to the action of the Bishops, but was brought about by the strong and natural feelings of the people. Muharram offers the same phenomenon by which the people themselves have developed orthodox doctrines in accordance with their own inner conviction.

In such cases the Hierarchy is compelled to sanction what it formally disapproves.

During the war, for example, all arms had to be handed over to the civil power, including the swords used for head-cutting at Muharram. Some days before the fast I had been discussing the approaching ceremonies with the Chief Mujtahid, who, as I have already mentioned, told me that all extreme forms of asceticism were strictly forbidden ('haram'); and that it was not officially possible to permit more than a slight striking of the breast, the devotee being fully clothed. Under the 'Arms Proclamation' the swords required were in my possession, and on the eighth of Muharram I received a verbal request from some Alim to hand them over to the bearer. After what I had been told, by authority, I felt justified in refusing; for who was I, a mere 'kafir', to cause an occasion of sin to the believer? I wrote a polite letter to His Holiness stating that, after our recent conversation, I could not comply with this request without a definite order from him, adding that, in consequence of the Arms Proclamation, his letter would have to state definitely that the swords were required for a religious ceremony only. I

SHIA' AND SUNNI

hoped, in the wickedness of my heart, that I had caught the old gentleman on the horns of a dilemma. I was requested, however, to hand over the swords; but though the letter bore the seal of His Holiness, he had carefully avoided signing it. The body of the document was in the handwriting of his secretary, who had signed without sealing!

On the material side, the Mujtahidun and Ulema are, naturally, influenced by a desire to retain their clientele. For this reason they yield to the popular demand for such religious expressions; and there can be little doubt that they will eventually become an authorised devout practice. The Mujtahid, however, still hesitates to issue a fatwah, lest such public approval might involve the writer himself, and his followers, in taking an active part!

There is an actual tradition that Hussein, before setting out for Kufa, prayed to Allah, saying, 'I am going to die for Thy people', and there can be no manner of doubt that this thought underlies the extravagance in mortification which is manifested during the ten days of Muharram, drawing bitter tears from those who are ordinarily self-contained. One cannot help comparing the effect produced on the audience when the story of the Battle of Kerbela is read, with that produced on Christians of Europe by the account of the Tragedy of Calvary.

But though this element of 'vicarious suffering', which is peculiarly developed in the Shia' of Iraq, owing to the presence of the Holy Cities, is so essentially a Christian conception, it may – on the other hand actually impede conversion. A little

THE INS AND OUTS OF MESOPOTAMIA

thought will show the reason. In the ordinary heathen land, where the only religion is some form of animism, where the predominant emotion governing conduct is fear, and where dread of evil spirits and the witch-doctor or medicine-man governs every action, the Gospel comes as very definite GOOD NEWS. It is absolutely GOOD and wholly NEW. True, much prejudice, many ancient customs and superstitions have to be overcome; but there is at any rate a natural subconscious desire to accept it, because in contrast with their own belief it is definitely desirable. The relief to an individual, who has passed his whole life in permanent dread of evil spirits, when he becomes convinced that fear is for ever replaced by love, cannot be realised.

But to the Shia' of Iraq this could not be said. It is not a case of bringing them NEWS of a Mediator, but of stating that He whom we regard as the only Mediator is BETTER than the Mediator whom they already know, and whom they love with a devotion that is greater than that usually shown to our Lord. This is a very different proposition. Moreover, to the savage animist, Jesus is an entire stranger. He comes as a glorious surprise. With the Shia', and especially in Iraq, He is already honoured as second only to the Prophet himself. Further, the corner-stone of Christianity is the Atonement of Calvary, which the Muslim denies with a certainty that can only come from the very word of God Himself – the Quran.

I shall be dealing later with the Islamic system in general, its rigidity, and the hopelessness of expecting any kind of progress from a people who

SHIA' AND SUNNI

profess this faith. If this is true of Islam in general, it is far more so of the Shia', Largely owing to the mystical elements that they have grafted into their belief, but more especially to the doctrine of 'taqiya', which may be understood as 'compromise'. The religious authority for this is found in verse 27 of Sura iii: 'Let not the believers take the unbelievers for friends rather than the believers; and whoever does this he shall have nothing of the guardianship of Allah, *but you should guard yourselves against them, guarding carefully.*'

The words in italics are the essence of the doctrine. The Sunnis declare that this verse only applied to the condition of affairs during the early days of Islam, but the Shia' practises them in his daily life.

It simply means that a 'religious' man may make any protestation of friendship with an unbeliever, may do anything to deceive him, may tell him any lie that can forward the deception. The result, of course, is that those who are religiously inclined have no moral sense.

The doctrine has eaten into all their relations with people of another faith, as may be seen from the following sentence in a letter that I received from one who had been a very real friend to me during my stay in the country. He was, when I knew him, thoroughly irreligious, not even observing the Fast of Ramadhan! He wrote: 'I am now become religious, but *none the less* I still want to see you.'

It will be easily understood that one can seldom depend on real friendship from a Shia'. I firmly believe it would be impossible from one who is, in his sense of the word, 'religious'. Remembering always that the Sunni is regarded by such a man as even lower than a 'kafir', it will be evident that any idea of a 'tauhid' (i.e. union) is a figment of the imagination.

CHAPTER VI

CRIME

Taxes by blackmail. Blood-money, and a vendetta. Complex land-tenure. The Law of Inheritance. Criminal types of three faiths. The brutal Kurd.

AS MAY BE EXPECTED, offences against the social order vary considerably in the tribes and in the towns. And, again, there is a distinction between the essentially tribal towns, the Holy Cities, and Baghdad. The tribal towns are very often simply markets for the barter of tribal produce, around which has grown up a small township, inhabited chiefly by petty merchants who are adepts in the art of extracting the uttermost from the woolly tribesmen. Many of these small townships have a unique system of policing which is very typical of the *laissez-faire*, albeit shrewd, methods employed by the Turks and backed up by the inhabitants. It is known as the Paswaniyah system, and is kept up by a Paswaniyah tax.

The Paswaniyah is a band of men composed of the most notable blackguards of the town and the surrounding tribes, whose organisation obviously discourages open crime, since their whereabouts must be well known. The Paswaniyah tax is thus

THE INS AND OUTS OF MESOPOTAMIA

seen to combine insurance with blackmail. Every person who desires to be secure from robbery, murder, and sudden death must pay. There is no compulsion, but in practice this tax is better 'supported' than any other municipal levy! There is no attempt to escape payment, but rather the reverse. For if a householder refuses to pay, his house is not protected, and he cannot expect to escape the burglar! The degree of security will be exactly determined by the amount paid to the leader of the Paswaniyah, *over and above the actual tax*.

It is not considered wise to complain of this system to the Government, for obvious reasons. It is purely a little private transaction between the parties concerned. The members of the Paswaniyah are on the whole fairly prosperous, and the competition for enrolment is, naturally, keen. A Government which has evolved an attractive service for criminals has indeed accomplished something notable. However, the Paswaniyah do not have it all their own way. The security they offer includes an undertaking to refund the value of all property that may be stolen whenever a burglary occurs. Now this condition produces some very piquant situations. 'Needless to say, the Paswaniyah always dispute the claim, and their line of argument is always the same, *that the appellant has robbed himself*. Where this is true, we recognise a simple way of making money, and there is not a shadow of doubt that in some cases it has been done.

On the lower Euphrates there is a tribe called the Jenabat, who are openly, and to a man, no other than professional thieves. They do not culti-

CRIME

vate or keep flocks, but they live very fairly well. From this tribe, the Paswaniyah for all the neighbouring towns and villages was recruited. In one particular town their extortions were becoming so unbearable that the inhabitants determined to resist their power, and a most astonishing epidemic of crime broke out. Burglary after burglary was reported, and arguments usually adopted by the Paswaniyah to avoid compensation were of no avail, because the burglaries had very obviously been committed from outside, by thieves breaking in during the night.

The Paswaniyah had to pay up in accordance with their contract, and they were completely broken up. Many months later it leaked out that several of the inhabitants had arranged to burgle each other's houses!

The activities of the Jenabat are not confined to membership of the Paswaniyah. They are exceedingly clever thieves, and work in many of the towns. They are particularly skilled in the gentle art of picking pockets, working in bands of four or five. The victim having been selected, A hustles him, B takes his purse, handing it to C, and he to D, who passes it on to E, with incredible rapidity. The victim may recognise both A and B, who are searched at their own request; but E meanwhile strolls off, and the band forgathers in a coffee-shop a few minutes later.

I have previously mentioned the 'fasl', or blood-money. Owing to this system it is comparatively rare for officials of an administration to hear of violent crime among the tribes. Every tribe has its own fixed price for a man or a woman, a boy or a girl. In some cases the value of a horse is considerably greater than that of a man. Crimes of violence among the tribes are not very frequent, and one can seldom hold one party more responsible than the other. Deliberately planned murder is almost unknown, except over a woman, and such cases are sufficiently startling.

The most interesting crime of this nature that I recall was a double murder which took place at Najaf, the victims being a money-changer, 'sarraf', and his wife. The bodies were discovered in the early morning. The house where they lived was on the usual plan; that is, a one-storey quadrangle surrounding a small courtyard, with a flat space outside the single upstairs room, from which the stairs led down into the courtyard.

The 'sarraf' was found half-way down the stairs, stabbed in eleven places. He had evidently been first attacked in the upstairs room, and finally disposed of as he was making his escape. There was blood everywhere, and the whole house was in a perfectly appalling condition. The wife was found in the cellar, with a wound fifteen inches long straight across the abdomen. For some reason, though she was fully clothed, her dress was entirely uninjured. After ten days' work on the case, fifteen people were arrested, one of whom confessed, and the motive of this mysterious crime became clear.

Twelve years previously the 'sarraf' had violated one of two sisters; she was almost immediately afterwards murdered by her own brothers, but the 'sarraf' had fled and completely disappeared. Do what they would, the brothers of the

CRIME

girl had been unable to trace him. They were conscripted by the Turks in the war: one was killed, and the other taken prisoner.

Revenge was not, however, allowed to drop, and two of the girl's uncles pursued the search for the guilty 'sarraf', who had hidden in Najaf under a different name, and taken a Najafi for his wife. One of the uncles now came on pilgrimage to the Holy City, and, though years had much altered the 'sarraf', the avenger at once recognised his victim. The second uncle, when summoned, confirmed his suspicions, and cautious inquiries of neighbours soon established the fact. Unfortunately for himself, the 'sarraf' did not recognise them, and it was an easy matter to obtain an introduction, pose as friends, and secure an invitation to his house, which enabled them to become thoroughly acquainted with his *ménage*. They were old men, apparently averse to personal violence; but through a friend, who was well acquainted with the surrounding tribes, they procured two tribesmen, who undertook to dispose of the 'sarraf' for the sum of five rupees, or 6s. 8d. each. Upon the night fixed the three actually conducted their hirelings to the house, and knocked at the door, which the woman opened. The tribesmen, of course, had no personal interest in the affair, but they had been paid to kill the man in this house, while their employers waited for them outside. When they came out to report themselves however, one of the uncles remembered the wife, who must also die, lest they were betrayed by her evidence. The younger murderer offered to go back, and easily silenced her in a few moments.

THE INS AND OUTS OF MESOPOTAMIA

The story may well serve to show the persistence of family feuds, and the amazingly low value of life among the tribes. These murderers were admittedly poor specimens, but the average is not much higher among the 'fellaliyeh', who will do almost anything for money. It is quite possible that these two had never before actually handled hard cash, and that the bribe represented immense wealth to their woolly brains. Finally, we see by what means the high standard of conjugal fidelity has been maintained by the Shia'. Retribution may be delayed, but it will most assuredly come!

The following case shows an interesting variation in tribal custom. A young Arab girl, Miriam, was greatly sought after by her cousin, but owing to a family quarrel, her father absolutely forbade the alliance. The family, with their accompanying tribesmen, were moving from place to place when they were suddenly raided by the cousin and three of his men, who carried off the girl right under her father's nose, one tribesman being killed and the brother of the girl wounded. Though Miriam's father took the unusual course of appealing to the Civil power, it was so clearly a case for settlement by tribal law that the Sheikh of the tribe was called, another Sheikh summoned to sit with him, and the matter was amicably arranged by the payment of 'fasl' for the killed and injured men, and the payment of dowry. However, what principally interested me in this case was the girl's embarrassment when asked to expose her face. It was quite impossible to hear what she said; but though her lover, father, and brother also ordered her to

CRIME

unveil, the most they could accomplish was the exposure of one eye!

Sexual morality is naturally very much higher in the tribes than in the towns. The 'fellaliyeh' lead a very hard life, in many cases literally from hand to mouth, and opportunity to transgress is almost non-existent.

As I have pointed out above, many criminal cases are settled by the Sheikhs, whose judgments are always respected if they have any hold over their tribesmen. Punishment is swift and severe. A case came to my knowledge in which sentence of death was passed, and the Sheikh shot the accused there and then in the tribal court! There can be no doubt about the fact, though I could never discover what crime had been committed.

I cannot leave the subject of tribal misdemeanour without mentioning the constant recurrence of 'Land cases', which, though not criminal in themselves, give enormous scope for innumerable acts of crime, such as forgery, perjury and general dishonesty. These cases, of course, do not in any way concern the 'fellaliyeh', but are always between the Sheikhs, their Sirakil, and the landowning Syeds. Land-tenure in Iraq is probably the most involved and hopeless affair imaginable, and I can think of nothing more typically Turkish in its incompetency and the impossibility of any practical application. It is known as Tapu, which some ingenious official stated was derived from the Greek 'topos', a place. The head office is in Baghdad, in which all title deeds to property are supposed to be kept; and the scheme is beautiful in theory. All land is supposed to be held by Government, and the people can only remain in occupation so long as they pay their revenue, which is regarded as rent. Land which is not Tapu is Miri, a conundrum which I could never fathom, but it is said to mean that the sole ownership is vested in the State. Clearly there should be in Baghdad a complete catalogue of all occupied land, and the revenue returns should be at least quadrupled. But unfortunately the Turkish officials forgot the necessity of mapping the country, and made no provision for the most corrupt officialdom in the world, in their head office. Sheikhs rolled up by the score to the metropolis. They were asked to define their own boundaries, and duly gave the required information – with a small solatium to the clerk who wrote up their title deeds. Therefore we have many deeds which read something as follows: 'On the north the rice fields of Haji Juwad, on the east the Persian mountains, on the south the Red Sea, and on the west the desert.' Such deeds were scattered broadcast over the land.

In addition to Tapu, there is the Muslim Law of Inheritance; and a most evil institution known as Waqf, about equally incomprehensible, which means land or property left for the support of religious institutions. The Muslim Law of Inheritance is far too complicated to define here but its complete theory or basis is laid down in the following verses of the Quran:

Sura iv. 11. Allah enjoins you concerning your children. The male shall have the equal of the portion of two females, then if there are more than two females, they shall have two-thirds of what the deceased has left, and if

CRIME

there is one she shall have the half; and as for his parents, each of them shall have the sixth of what he has left if he has a child, but if he has no child and only his two parents inherit him then his mother shall have the third; but if he has brothers, then his mother shall have the sixth after the payment of any bequest that he may have bequeathed or a debt; your parents and your children, you know not which is the nearer to you in usefulness; this is an ordinance from Allah; surely Allah is Knowing, Wise.

12. And you shall have half of what your wives leave if they have no child, but if they have a child then you shall have a fourth of what they leave after payment of any bequest they may have bequeathed or a debt; and they shall have the fourth of what you leave if you have no child, but if you have a child, then they shall have the eighth of what you leave after payment of any bequest you may have bequeathed or a debt; and if a man or a woman leave property to be inherited by neither parents nor offspring and he or she has a brother or a sister, then each of the two shall have the sixth, but if they are more than that, they shall be sharers in the third after payment of any bequest that may have been bequeathed or a debt that does not harm others; this is an ordinance from Allah, and Allah is Knowing, Forbearing. These are Allah's limits.

(There is also a later revelation, which supplements the foregoing.)

177. Allah gives you a decision concerning the person who has neither parents nor offspring; if a man dies and he has no son and he has a sister she shall have half of what he leaves, and he shall be her heir if she shall have no son; but if there be two sisters they shall have two-thirds of what he leaves; and if there are brethren, men and women, then the male shall have the like of the portion of two females; Allah makes clear to you (!) lest you err.

THE INS AND OUTS OF MESOPOTAMIA

I hope that the reader now fully understands what the Law of Inheritance really is. Consider, for example, the head of a large and wealthy family with estates in different parts of the country, including gardens and town property. He dies, and the calculation begins. Meanwhile, another member of the same family dies, which throws out the original calculation. And so it goes on. Consider finally that every one of the title deeds on which these calculations are based is utterly and totally valueless, and you have some idea of the opportunities which any land-suit can provide. Remembering the avarice of the Arab, can any system be imagined which would give more chances of 'grab', and all the evils that 'grab' is heir to? Altogether, apart from the almost limitless opportunities for forgery, the truth of things is further hidden by the corruption of the erstwhile officials who naturally receive fees to stick to their original lie.

Consider the amount of ill-feeling that this Law of Inheritance must, and in fact does, produce. The Quran tells us 'These are Allah's limits.' We are thankful He went no further!

The Zuweini case, famed throughout the world of Islam, was only typical of many. The land involved made up about twenty square miles of most valuable date gardens, and its possession had been disputed before the Shara' Court for over seventy years, while naturally all deaths in the family were continually confusing the issue. It would be difficult to say off-hand how much crime had entered into the case. When it came to my knowledge the different parties hated each other far

CRIME

more than they hated even the Sunni. For the nth time it came before the Shara'; but now for the first time a British Administration was in charge, and (though even the Chief Mujtahid was intimidated and reversed his first decision) at long last the Court made its final decision. The practical administration of the judgment fell to my lot to supervise, and was eventually accomplished after the most incalculable difficulty. During the course of the final settlement, two most curious and unaccountable deaths occurred in the family of one of the chief parties to the action, but there was no evidence to proceed upon. The Law of Inheritance, the existence of the Mujtahidun, and the system of Tapu, form a trinity which would damn for ever the most enlightened nation in the world. Jarndyce *v*. Jarndyce is nothing to it.

'These are Allah's limits.' Thank God!

There is everything against the Arab in Iraq, and it can only be due to the innate sterling worth of his nature that he survives with so many genuine and lovable qualities.

Naturally crime wears a different aspect in Baghdad and other large towns, but I do not think it is materially worse than in most Western cities.

The religious and racial characteristics of this composite population show a marked difference in motive and method. The following two native murders, one Jewish and the other Christian, afford an interesting comparison with the Muslim murder already recounted.

Ishaq was an old man of about eighty years. He was a striking figure, over six feet, slightly bowed, with a thin, beaked nose, luxuriant eyebrows, and

THE INS AND OUTS OF MESOPOTAMIA

a long, silky, grey beard. His family consisted of his wife, two daughters, and his son Eliahoo. The elder daughter, about thirty-three years old, was an hysterical creature, subject to melancholia. She also showed tendencies in her relationship with the other sex which were the reverse of desirable, though there was no direct evidence of actual immorality. The old gentleman, claiming direct descent from the Prophet Aaron, was rightly proud of his name, and jealous of his family honour. He and his son Eliahoo gravely conferred upon the best means of removing this appalling disgrace. As no milder measures seemed to promise a safe way, the two men deliberately trapped their victim into an empty room, on the pretence of desiring some private conversation, knocked her down, put a long scarf round her neck, and both pulled, one at each end. The father, in his subsequent confession, affirmed that she took about half an hour to die. To him, certainly, it must have seemed so. The horror and pathos of the scene staggers imagination, when the age, relationship, and the victim of the murder are considered. Let it be remembered that the old father was, all the time, really devoted to his daughter, but his family honour seemed to him above all. Having murdered the girl, they brought her body out into the courtyard of the house. The other daughter had been left in ignorance of this grim family council. Her mother, who knew all, kept her talking upstairs, and when she now stepped out on to the balcony, so that her sister's corpse lay, as it were, at her feet, she, too, went mad.

CRIME

The house was right in the middle of the Jewish quarter of Baghdad, and it was in removing the body, that the crime came to light. The father and son first buried it about a foot down, under the kitchen floor; but the heat soon showed them that it would be impossible to escape discovery by such a means. Eliahoo therefore went out and arranged with two Muslims, for the sum of 2,000 rupees, that they should carry it to the river by night. Eliahoo then disappeared, and has never been seen since, but the old man followed this gruesome funeral, weeping bitterly for his daughter.

They were stopped by a night-watchman, the two Muslims ran away, and Ishaq, overcome with grief and nervous prostration, confessed the whole story. It is almost impossible to believe that family and racial pride could be carried to such extreme lengths. The willing participation of the son, and the agreement of the mother, are most suggestive and enlightening. The loyalty of the second daughter, who was able to appear at the trial, was also very striking. Her one idea was to protect her father, who, of course, denied altogether that his confession was genuine. None would desire to mitigate so unnatural a crime; but it, nevertheless, also reveals an element of fine courage and utter self-immolation on the altar of family honour.

In the second case, Tobias, a Chaldean Christian, aged about thirty-five, came down with his mother from Mosul to Baghdad for a few days' holiday. He was tolerably well off, and on the night of his arrival made his way to the prostitutes' quarter. One of the unfortunate women who lived there was named Fatima, who, as it appeared in evidence, could both read and write, was exceedingly clever and witty, and generous to a fault. She had become a prostitute when quite a child through no fault of her own, and spent her life in bringing as much happiness as possible into the lives of her miserable sisters. To Fatima went Tobias. Now the wealth of these women is largely comprised in necklaces made of solid gold, on which are suspended a large quantity of golden liras. Bangles stretching from wrist to elbow, and anklets from foot to knee are also worn. Fatima was more than usually well provided with these ornaments. Tobias, having passed the night with her, woke up in the early morning and cut her throat. He found that her ornaments were too small to get over her hands and feet, so he cut off these members, and, putting the bangles in his pocket, went home and handed them to his mother. They were found distributed about her person, when both were arrested.

I have selected these three cases of murder because each one is in its way characteristic. Neither the first nor the second were regarded as sinful by the perpetrators themselves. Both were in a sense altruistic. The first was to avenge the family honour, long since besmirched; the second was to prevent the family honour being besmirched. The third speaks for itself. Sheer wanton brutality or treachery like this is not part of the Arab character. There are, naturally, exceptions, but I never personally came across this characteristic. Gruesome stories, probably true, are extant of individuals having been found during our advance up the Tigris, who had been cut open by the Arabs. But

CRIME

such deeds were not prompted by mere wanton brutality. The Turks, when they were retreating, cut open many Arabs, to discover whether they had swallowed any gold liras; and the example once given, the Arab followed suit, for the same reason. For general brutality and villainy we have to go to the Kurds, who are very numerous in Baghdad. It is no exaggeration to say that over 50 per cent of the crime committed in that city can be traced to the Kurd. A more untrained savage it would be hard to find. The brutalities inflicted on our soldiers after the surrender of the Kut garrison were committed by Kurds. Most of the Armenian massacres were carried out by the Kurds, at the instigation of the Turk. The latter know that murder, loot, and rape are the natural activities of these gentry.

The writer quoted below is well acquainted with that particular race, and has been in most intimate touch with them for many years. His judgment in such matters is beyond question.

The following is an extract from a letter I received a short time ago:

'Awful news from Suleimani; two of the best gone West. Both of them shot in the back – typical of the Kurd. Also a serious rising said to be going on, Suleimani surrounded and generally hell to pay. I am probably just as well out of it, for I didn't like the Kurd and would probably have booted somebody at a critical political moment. I am sorry for the boys that are there, but we owe the trouble largely, I believe, to the policy of that amiable idealist —, with his theories of the "noble Kurd", etc., *ad nauseam*.

THE INS AND OUTS OF MESOPOTAMIA

The mailed fist and the heavy stick are the only things among people who stab in their own "madhifs", and who waylay the guest on his way to their guest-house, who sell their wives to the wayfarer for five rupees and whose religion is a thing of horror. That is why I would never have a Kurdish servant sleep in my house and why I imported Arabs at heavy expense, for I knew, at least, that I could sleep without a "khanjar" (dagger) in the back from my own household.

I knew the Kurd from Rowan-duz days, which very few did, and I knew him for what he is, and I spoke like Cassandra to the Trojans.

"Fine upstanding men, the Kurds"; "God's gentlemen"; "Men of the hills living in God's pure air"; "Men of simple life and simple virtues". Such were the replies that I received to my warnings. Possibly it is now realised why Suleimani cannot be the hill-station for wives and families from Baghdad, but it has cost us the lives of four good British officers to make it clear to the intelligences of the authorities, including —, who became positively "sloppy" over the "simple Arcadian life" on her two days' visit to Suleimani.'

It is an enlightening extract from many points of view, and I can vouch from my own experience, that everything in it is perfectly true. I would wish to make clear that where, in this book, I refer to the Muslim, I do not include the Kurd, although that is his official religion. He is beyond the pale. There let us leave him.

Adjudicating in a criminal court for a year gives one a valuable insight into local character, and nothing struck me more than the deteriorating effect of town life on the Arab. Even so, his peculiar

CRIME

characteristics were quite distinctive. His greed to amass money, for example, would be intensified by the town environment, but still shows itself in childish impulsive desire to injure his rival, without a thought of any ultimate advantage. To put it more concretely, A would quarrel with B about a piece of land. The quarrel would not confine itself to this subject for more than thirty seconds. Side-issue after side-issue would be brought in, the supporters of either side would shriek themselves hoarse, until finally a knife or a heavy stick would settle the affair. Then, when it was all over, the original land question would be settled by mutual adjustment (for these quarrels are seldom lasting), or by the weaker party giving in to the stronger. Whereas the original cause of the quarrel was the land, the cause of the blow might have been anything – quite likely an insult rather more prurient than usual.

Avarice, as I have already often remarked, can be found in all strata of society, but among the Muslims it is most common in the upper classes. And they acquire the other man's goods – if I may use the term – in a far more gentlemanly spirit than we find among the indigenous Christians or Jews. The following incident could not have happened among Muslims – not even in town!

Thoma, a Christian, had two sons, eighteen and sixteen years respectively. After the capture of Baghdad they were penniless and starving, but Thoma had a small mill. A Christian woman, who had been a friend of the family for more than twenty years, came to the rescue, and lent him 5,000 rupees in return for a third share in the fu-

THE INS AND OUTS OF MESOPOTAMIA

ture profits, up to the 5,000 rupees and 10 per cent interest. When the first instalment became due, the younger son went to the woman's house late one evening, and told her that his father had the money ready, if she would bring round the document to be endorsed with the date of the first payment. She accordingly fetched the document and set forth with the younger son. He then led her by a 'short cut' through a dark lane, where she was set upon by the elder son. The two boys snatched her paper and ran away in the darkness. She had, of course, no other evidence of the original transaction, and had not a passer-by seen the attack, by pure chance, she could not possibly have obtained redress.

It is true that Christians were not often charged with serious offences, but there are not many of our faith in Baghdad, and whenever they did appear there was an element of contemptible meanness in the crime rarely found among Muslims, and not often among the Jews.

On the other hand, the following case shows how well the Muslim understands his 'brother' Jew!

An ancient Jew, Moshi by name, was a moneychanger. He did his business at a street corner, squatting on the pavement, a handkerchief spread out in front of him, covered with neat little piles of liras, rupees, krans, and other currencies. One Friday evening he gathered up his stock, totalling about Rs.7,000 mostly in notes, and was making his way home. Muhammad Ali, a youth of nineteen, suddenly leapt upon the old man and, slipping a knife into his neck, demanded the bag of coin and notes. Moshi yelled, but hung on to the bag, till Muhammad Ali gave him another dig, and this time secured his booty. But Moshi's yells had attracted a crowd, and some ten people – all Jews – set off in pursuit and were soon joined by others. Muhammad Ali was about twenty yards ahead, and behind him a rapidly increasing pack. The quarry knew that his pursuers were all Jews, so he dropped a note of Rs.100. The crowd behind stopped so suddenly, and the scramble for the note was so great, that they all fell over one another. Thus Muhammad rapidly gained on his pursuers, and every time the chase got too hot, he dropped some more cash. The pursuers slowly diminished in numbers, until at last the bag was exhausted. Had the thief not been so unfortunate as to run down a cul-de-sac, he would undoubtedly have got clear away.

In petty crime, such as 'drunk and disorderly', the culprits were almost invariably Jews or Christians, with a large preponderance of Jews. Cases of street gambling were fairly frequent, but the Jews were generally the guilty parties. Muslims occasionally would be found gambling in the coffee-shops, and small boys of both religions in the streets.

There is, of course, no doubt that the dancing girls of the theatres were great inciters to crime. They were almost entirely Jewesses. One or two Christians were latterly brought over from Beyrout and Aleppo.

One most striking fact is that during the whole year only one case was brought before me of a servant stealing from his master, and in this case the

THE INS AND OUTS OF MESOPOTAMIA

master was entirely to blame. There were cases, of course, in which summary discipline had been dealt out on the spot, but I have no hesitation in saying that the Arab servant is a much more honest proposition than his brother of Hindustan.

CHAPTER VII

CONJUGAL RELATIONSHIP AND DIVORCE

Teaching compared with practice. Greater laxity in 'interpreting' the Quran among the Shia'. Concubinage and the 'temporary marriage'. Demoralising to manhood. Customs and ceremonies. The dowry. *Official* restrictions to divorce largely ignored. Moral depravity of the Holy Cities. Anecdote of wife-beating.

THIS IS A COMPLICATED subject and we must first examine the official teaching laid down in the Quran, which, naturally, forms the basis of all local usages. That polygamy is permitted is well known, though the circumstances under which the already existing system was confirmed are not usually taken into account. The authority is found in Sura iv. 3:

'And if you fear that you cannot act equitably towards orphans, then marry such women as seem good to you, two and three and four; but if you fear that you will not do justice between them, then marry only one, or what your right hand possesses; this is more proper that you may not deviate from the right course.'

Though the orthodox, i.e. the Sunni, consider that this verse gives permission for four wives, yet the circumstance of this 'revelation' clearly shows that it was actually granted for the sake of orphans. The Quran is made up of these sudden 'revelations', which conveniently made their appearance as circumstances seemed to demand them. In this particular case a battle had been fought, and many of the faithful had been killed. In order that the women and children might be properly looked after – and the wastage of life made good – this verse was revealed. The Sunni is particular as to four wives and no more, but the Shia' has interpreted the matter differently. The term, 'what your right hand possesses', is taken by them to authorise concubinage, and the households of Iraq tribal chiefs, more especially the wealthy land-owning Syeds, are astonishing and immense.

It is considered a great honour by the common folk if a daughter of their family is taken into the household of a Syed, a direct descendant of the Prophet. The advantages are not confined to this life, but they will also have a friend at Court, when the days of the holy man come to an end. The result is astounding. Ancient and decrepit old men, who are entitled to the green turban, will be found in possession of young girls of fifteen, who, the legal quota of four wives being complete, are not married, but live with them as concubines.

The following story is well authenticated of a respected and most holy Syed, whom I know personally very well. He is a short, stout old boy, about seventy years old, an empty barrel, who, with the aid of spectacles resting obliquely across his face and an air of inscrutable wisdom, will

CONJUGAL RELATIONSHIP AND DIVORCE

utter platitudes by the hour together, which are regarded by his followers as evidence of the profoundest thought. He was the leading spirit of the revolution of 1920, was indirectly responsible for many murders of British Officers, but made his escape at the end. He was subsequently invited back to the country by the British Administration and duly arrived, as the confidant of Feisal, the Amir imposed upon the people by our Colonial Office for reasons which will subsequently be made clear!

This Syed was one day sitting in his 'madhif', surrounded by many leading Sheikhs and sycophants, burbling inanities to the usual admiring audience, in this case numbering about seventy souls. In the middle of one of his most telling orations, a small boy of four years came toddling up the centre of the 'madhif', and put his arms round the great man's neck. He was angrily flung off.

'Who are you?' demanded the Syed.

'Your son', lisped the small child, who was at once hastily removed by a retainer.

This worthy old gentleman had, of course, his four wives, and, I am credibly informed, thirty-nine concubines!

The system obviously explains the enmity frequently noticed between brothers, sons of the same father, but by different wives or concubines; and naturally family unity is thereby utterly undermined. The children by a wife take precedence over those by concubines; but, if the father is a Syed, all his male offspring become Syeds in their turn.

THE INS AND OUTS OF MESOPOTAMIA

It is in his marriage system that the Shia' has made the most striking departures from the orthodox usage of the Sunni. He not only sanctions concubinage, but has established the 'mu'ta', or temporary marriage, which permits a man and a woman to live together as man and wife for a definitely stated period. The period is named on the agreement, and the dowry paid over as in an ordinary marriage. When the period has expired there is no obligation on either side. It may be renewed or not, as the parties agree. In this case, divorce is not permitted, and any children that may arise from the 'marriage' accrue to the husband.

The orthodox, following the rule of the Khaliph Omar, rightly regard this system with extreme disgust, and it is one of the chief reasons which render union between the two great divisions impossible.

It will easily be seen that the Shia' has made life as easy as possible from the point of view of sensual enjoyment. Since only the wealthy can permanently afford four wives, the poor are compensated by the system of 'mu'ta', and can enjoy a life of uncontrolled libertinism, at a comparatively cheap rate.

It will surely not be disputed that family life is the base of all social development, and therefore of ordered government and national consciousness. The people, who have had these systems in force for hundreds of years, are now asked by enlightened Europe what kind of Government they desire, on the ground that they have the right to govern themselves as they wish. If they would only first learn to govern themselves individually, these

CONJUGAL RELATIONSHIP AND DIVORCE

idealistic aspirations might not seem so absurd. The more this custom is looked into, the more utterly fatal it is seen to be. The marriage system not only degrades the women of the race and dishonours motherhood, but its effects are no less enervating and deadly upon the men – who at present possess all the political power; and it attacks with especial force just that class of the great and wealthy who are in power and would remain there under self-government. Consider the life of the young heir, destined, as some would have him, to control his country's fate. He is brought up among fawning, uneducated, and sensual women, whose whole purpose in life must be to retain their physical attractions for their lord and master, who cannot escape petty jealousies, and have no thought or care beyond the gratification of idle and luxurious taste. There is no change for him in manhood, save from a petted plaything to the flattered lord and master of his own women, in his own home.

'In youth it must be ruin to be petted and spoiled by a company of submissive slave-girls. In manhood it is no less an evil that when a man enters into private life his affections should be put up to auction among foolish fond competitors full of mutual jealousies and slanders. We are not left entirely to conjecture as to the effect of female influence in home life when it is exerted under unenlightened and demoralising conditions. That is plainly an element *lying at the root of all the most important features that differentiate progress from stagnation.*'

Clearly, it is the chief leaders of society who have been brought up in this way. They are the ultimate strength of the country, into whose hands power would fall, should 'self-government' become an accomplished fact.

The ceremony of marriage in Iraq, except for the variations already noted, is the same as in other Muslim lands. The preliminary arrangements are carried out by a female relative of the prospective bridegroom, who is soon ready with her list of the most suitable girl-candidates. The bridegroom's family then discuss the matter with him from every possible point of view. If the family is poor the girl will have to come and live in their house, and though the bridegroom naturally regards her looks as of chief importance, his family will consider that other qualities require a closer investigation.

Much will depend upon her capacity for all household duties, her abilities as a cook, her temper, and her price. The question of the dowry naturally limits the choice, and her family must be at least as good as the bridegroom's, for pride of birth is a very strong sentiment in Arab psychology. Gradually those who are considered unsuitable, from one point of view or another, are eliminated, and the final decision may rest between two or three.

Then comes the inspection by the mother, sister, or aunt of the bridegroom. They are invited to the girl's house, and the prospective bride will be on duty, i.e. she will hand round sweetmeats, tea, coffee, and sherbet, her movements about the room giving her every opportunity of displaying her figure, her graceful carriage, and her general charm. She is dressed in her best, and has probably adorned herself with bangles and anklets borrowed from her family for the occasion. Should this inspection prove satisfactory, the final negotiations are opened over the dowry, which is a matter for the males of the two families.

Travellers have found much to say against this system, which they describe, with a sneer, as 'buying one's wife as one might buy cattle'. But personally I can see little, or no difference between the method of Islam and the marriage settlements of Christian Europe. Both are given with the same idea, that the bride may start her married life with some secured property of her own, and in Islam, as elsewhere, this is of the greatest value to the wife in the event of a divorce. There is certainly much haggling and bargaining among the Arabs, but that is a national characteristic seen in all their transactions. Among the Euphrates tribes a really pretty and accomplished girl of good family will cost the bridegroom about £120. The 'cheapest' wife that I ever heard of was purchased for thirty rupees, that is, about £1 10s., at the then rate of exchange. I forbore from any inquiries as to her character or capacities!

Marriage in Islam is a duty compulsory on every male, and, like everything he must do, is ordained in the Quran. The directions as to the dowry are equally clear.

Sura iv. 4 reads:

'And give women their dowries as a free gift, but if they themselves be pleased to give up to you a portion of it, then receive it with enjoyment and wholesome result', and lest forcible persuasion may be employed, so that they may 'be pleased to give up a portion of it', there is added in verse 19 of the same Sura:

'Do not straiten them in order that you may take part of what you have given them, unless they are guilty of manifest indecency.'

The Prophet's knowledge of the avarice of his followers is well shown in the verse that follows. For if 'manifest indecency' is a justifiable reason to take part of the dowry away, a husband in need of ready cash might well accuse his wife of such indecency, and thereby force her to hand it over lest her honour be brought into disrepute. Therefore the Prophet adds:

'And if you wish one wife in place of another, and you have given one of them a heap of gold, then take not from it anything; would you take it by slandering her, and doing her manifest wrong?'

We will now consider the subject of Divorce in Islam. Here, again, the actual practice has departed in a great measure from that laid down in the Quran, which must be first set down. The causes for divorce are undefined and unlimited, but may be summed up in the word 'incompatibility'.

But before a divorce is accomplished, there are many conditions to be fulfilled, at least in a marriage that has been consummated. There is no such thing as separation without divorce, though a period must elapse before the decree of divorce be-

CONJUGAL RELATIONSHIP AND DIVORCE

comes finally effective, when the husband and wife live apart, so far as conjugal relationship is concerned, but remain under the same roof. It might be considered as a 'divorce nisi'. Divorce must be pronounced twice, and after each pronouncement a period of three months must elapse. The form used is 'I repudiate', which is said before witnesses. The reason for these two periods is threefold. Primarily it allows time for possible pregnancy to declare itself. Secondarily, it gives time for any disagreement to be adjusted between the parties. Thirdly, as a result of the first two, it acts as a check to promiscuous divorce.

Sura iv. 229 declares that 'divorce may be pronounced twice', that is, for a decree that has not been made absolute. Maulvi Muhammad Ali, in commenting on this, says:

'In the days of ignorance a man used to divorce his wife and take her back within the prescribed time, even though he might do this a thousand times. Islam reformed this practice by allowing a revocable divorce twice, so that the period of waiting in each of these two cases might serve as a period of temporary separation, during which conjugal relationship could be re-established.'

At the end of the second period, the man must finally decide whether he *is* going to divorce his wife or not. If he decides to retain her, he does so for good, and can never again divorce her save for gross immorality.

When the wife is finally divorced, it is absolutely forbidden for her husband to keep any part of her dowry. Remembering the money-loving nature of the Arab, the salutary effect of this law is obvious. It also serves to protect the woman, as she will not enter the world penniless.

The possession of the dowry also provides the woman with a powerful weapon, should she desire a divorce; for by giving up a portion to her husband, she can compel him to divorce her.

When the irrevocable decree of divorce has been pronounced, i.e. the third pronouncement, remarriage between the pair is impossible, except under one very peculiar condition, laid down in verse 230:

'So if he (the first husband) divorces her, she shall not be lawful to him afterwards until she marries another husband; and then if he (the second husband) divorces her, there is no blame on them both if they (the woman and the first husband) return to each other by marriage, if they think that they can keep within the limits of Allah' (i.e. perform the *debitum conjugale*).

The *official* teaching of Islam, therefore, while permitting divorce, hedges it round with restrictions and conditions which, if they were observed, would render it of comparatively rare occurrence. That it should have been authoritatively permitted at all, was doubtless due to the political necessities of the time. Several years of constant fighting necessarily involved many casualties, and, if the Prophet wished not only to hold the territory that he had already acquired, but to extend it, he had to make provision for an increase in his fighting force, and at the same time make the conditions of his faith sufficiently attractive to the character of

CONJUGAL RELATIONSHIP AND DIVORCE

the Arab to ensure new recruits. It was therefore essential that every impediment to free conjugal relationship should be removed.

It is interesting to compare Muslim lands with Christian countries in this connection. In the former we have the official permission of the religion of the country accorded to the practice. In the official religion of Christian countries it is absolutely and irrevocably forbidden, separation only being permitted, and that only for adultery. Yet additional judges have to sit in the Christian courts of our Christian country, in order to clear off the waiting-list of undefended divorce suits!

The actual practice in Mesopotamia is very different from Quranic teaching. This is mainly due to the temporary marriage system already mentioned, but very largely also to ignorance.

Grown men cannot answer the simplest questions as to their faith, and, if rebuked, merely say that they are not religious. They all know that the Quran is LITERALLY the actual words of God written down via Gabriel, by the Prophet, and they know that in that book certain things are broadly permitted and certain things forbidden. Among the former is divorce.

The women sometimes rebel against the sudden decision of their husbands, and appeal by a petition to the Government, who sends them to the Shara', or religious court. If the Hakim al Shara', i.e. the president, be an honest man, the parties will then learn, for the first time, that there are certain regulations which have to be observed.

Their ignorance on religious matters in general is well illustrated by an experience which happened to me in the 'madhif' of a certain rather wild and woolly Sheikh of a tribe, which had its habitat among the marshes. It was, however, a fairly large tribe, and the Sheikh himself wielded a good deal of power. We were sitting in the 'madhif' on a winter's evening. There were a good many other Arabs present, and we were discussing differences in social customs, etc., when the Sheikh said to me:

'Have I your permission to ask a question?'

(I will omit all the terms of address with which each sentence was plentifully besprinkled, terms such as 'your honour', 'your excellency', and, when referring to himself, 'your slave' or 'your servant'.)

Self. 'Yes, certainly.'

Sheikh. 'You will not be angry?'

S. 'No.'

Sh. 'Are you married?'

S. 'Yes.'

Sh. 'Why is your wife not with you?'

S. 'In wartime we may not bring women with us.'

Sh. 'That is a wise rule, but very difficult. It is not good for you to live alone.'

S. 'Perhaps not, but what can I do?'

Sh. 'Let me find a wife for you.'

S. (distinctly embarrassed). 'Thank you very much, but I fear that is impossible.'

Sh. 'Not at all. I can find you one, pretty and young, who will cook well; and you will be in every way much more comfortable.'

S. 'I fully appreciate your kindness, but my religion forbids us to have two wives.'

CONJUGAL RELATIONSHIP AND DIVORCE

Sh. 'Yes, perhaps so, but now you haven't got *one*!'

S. 'Yes, I have, but she is in England.'

Sh. 'I know; but you haven't got one here, and that is what I mean.'

S. 'But I shall some day return to England, and what shall I do then?'

Sh. 'Then you will divorce your Arab wife. She would not object; and perhaps, if you will let me find one for you, you will not leave us.'

It was with no little difficulty that I finally persuaded him to relinquish his idea, which had met with the greatest approval from the others present. The fact that marriage between a believer and a 'kafir' is absolutely forbidden was quite news to him; and he assured me that if that was really the case, it could easily be put right – presumably by a fat bribe to the Ulema!

Two officers whom I knew intimately had a similar experience. Doubtless this Sheikh imagined, at the back of his mind, that a marriage alliance between the Governor and his tribe would bring many advantages to him personally in such small details as the assessment of revenue; but the point of interest is that the offer was a genuine one, that a proper marriage as opposed to concubinage was intended, although his own religion absolutely forbade it. I should not care to think what the Religious Hierarchy in Najaf might have said in the matter had I fallen in with the suggestion!

With all the official facilities provided for sexual intercourse among the cultivating tribes, it is natural to find that there is no prostitution, except among a few wandering bands of so-called Darwish. The ordinary towns, however, like Baghdad and Hillah and others, have their special quarters for prostitutes, which they may never leave without a special pass from the police. In the Holy Cities, where the exceedingly severe penalties for fornication would probably quite literally be enforced, such women are never to be found. Occasionally a few make their way into Najaf under the guise of pilgrims, but are immediately expelled.

Here conjugal fidelity, so far as adultery in its strict sense is concerned, is strictly observed, owing to the prompt and drastic punishment of all offenders. But the Holy Cities contain about as choice a collection of degenerates as it would be possible to imagine. A negligible fraction of the inhabitants can read or write so that their 'relaxation' can only consist in gossiping in the coffee-shops, going to private 'kaifs', small parties where dancing-boys entertain the company, which are officially 'haram', drunkenness, and sexual orgies. The inevitable result is a most distressing prevalence of homosexuality, and even bestiality.

A very important and influential tribal Sheikh, who was noted for his piety and his blind devotion to the Hierarchy in Najaf and the sanctity of the city itself, was one day discussing with me the future education of his son.

I suggested sending him to the school that had just been opened in Najaf, which would involve his residence there with relatives. He replied: 'In some cities in this country 50 per cent of the boys are corrupt, but in Najaf 150 per cent. I would rather

CONJUGAL RELATIONSHIP AND DIVORCE

kill my son with my own hand than send him to live in Najaf.'

To ignore these unsavoury facts would leave a wrong impression on the minds of those who desire to really understand the social life of the Holy Cities and the sort of influence which radiates from them. When we remember that it is the rulers of these Holy Cities who are the real power in the whole country, who also mould the opinions of the tribal Sheikhs, one is literally aghast at the thought of such people having any say in the matter of their government.

To have relieved them from the tyranny of the Turk would be a small matter, if we leave them under the tyranny of their own 'Holy Men', with full opportunity to promulgate their revolting doctrines of temporary marriage, and concubinage, resulting in an ever-increasing degeneracy and ineptitude.

The following incident throws a strange light on the home-life of Shia' Islam. A certain Political Officer, filled with the idea of chivalry and the sacredness of womanhood, was, early in his career, presented with a petition from a heavily-veiled female which moved him profoundly. It was to the effect that she, Fatima, having no other protector than Almighty God and himself, had fled to him for succour. She was a married woman, who had borne her husband no less than five children, and had then been brutally turned out of her house. She had tried to return, not only to see her children, but also to collect some of her household goods, and had been set upon by her husband and most soundly beaten.

THE INS AND OUTS OF MESOPOTAMIA

The worthy officer was most profoundly moved. He understood little Arabic at the time, but sufficient to know that he had before him an unfortunate victim of wife-beating. He was determined to make an example, and show these wretched Arabs that if there was one thing more than another that the British Government would NOT stand, it was wife-beating. The husband was summoned and asked what the devil he meant by such brutality. The interpreter tried hard to explain that the woman was a thoroughly bad lot, who had actually been divorced many months back for the crime of barrenness, and that the husband held a most unimpeachable bill of divorcement from the Shara' Court and had never seen the woman since the decree, until that very moment. But our friend would hear no excuse: he had before him that most degenerate type of human being, the wife-beater, and passed sentence of three months' hard labour.

Had the Prophet himself suddenly risen up in the bazaar of the town, it could not have caused a greater sensation. There was not a doubt that madness had smitten their Hakim. Such was the common gossip in the coffee-shops. It was appalling. The whole of their social life was in a moment undermined. Had not the Prophet himself (and on him be the peace) laid it down in the Quran that unruly wives were to be beaten? The fact that in this particular case the whole charge was trumped up, did not worry them at all. The question was: 'When and how often has each of us beaten his own wife, and will she also send up a petition, and shall we ourselves be doing three months' hard labour? Furthermore, how can we possibly keep a

CONJUGAL RELATIONSHIP AND DIVORCE

semblance of discipline among our women when such things may happen?'

The interpreter, of course, waxed quite wealthy by means of promises to destroy any such appeals before they reached the Hakim. However, the unfortunate officer found himself snowed under with petitions from the wives of those who had not had the foresight to interview the interpreter. The same punishment was meted out to all, and consternation was everywhere.

But Allah is All Merciful, and in this case He smote the Hakim with an attack of malaria. None the less he made his way down to the office, though his head was bursting.

It was in the middle of the hot weather. The river flowed past the entrance to his office, and the door was kept open for any breeze that might enter. He sank down in his chair, and told the interpreter that he could not see any petitions except those of women who might want his assistance to relieve them of maltreatment. He was really very charitable, considering that his head was opening and shutting with throbs that seemed to be shooting in every direction at once.

A woman came in.

An excitable woman of any race is at normal times a trial, but when that woman is an Arab suffering under a grievance she is a yelling fury, and it is well not to have a headache at such moments. Such a woman was the petitioner. She came in accompanied by her husband, a most inoffensive and insignificant little man. She began to complain, and within a minute she was a raging tornado. Words poured forth, her voice rising higher and higher each moment, till she reached the highest possible note on which she could enunciate, and from that moment the office was filled with one continuous shriek. The Hakim held his splitting head. He groaned, and muttered little exclamations to the interpreter, 'Stop her, for God's sake, stop her!' Unavailing efforts were used. True, she stopped for a moment, but it was only to gain more strength to impress the Hakim with the justice of her case. He, poor man, was by this time barely conscious. His temperature was anything up to 104, weird lights were dancing before his eyes. His whole body seemed to be burnt up with the cataclysm that was going on in his head. She paused a moment. He looked up. He spoke. 'Oh Hell! chuck her in the river!' were his first audible words. The husband, of course, thought they were the dreaded sentence; and trembling he asked what the Governor had said. The interpreter gave a literal rendering. There was a shout of 'Al hamdu Lillah';[1] a confused mass appeared before the eyes of the Hakim; a mass of struggling draperies and shrieks – followed by a significant splash and silence. Great was the rejoicing in the coffee-shops that night. The short reign of feminine power was over, and it was universally agreed that the Prophet was most emphatically and surely the Apostle of God!

[1] Praise be to God.

CHAPTER VIII

THE SYSTEM

Influence of the Quran on national life and character. Opposition to schools. Hatred between sects. Whence comes the power of Islam? Hindu and Muslim leagued to 'set back' the world. Impervious to missionary effort. Christian teaching and practice compared. Power of religious tyranny and of faith in the 'divine' Imams. Flagrant perjury. 'Expiation' and 'Taqiya'. Muhammad's 'prudent' teaching. Unity (?) and self-government.

IT HAS BEEN SAID – and rightly – that every Muslim is a missionary. How is this possible, in view of their general ignorance? How can we account for the strength of Islam in spite of the fact that, from another point of view, it is a failure?

In the first place, the essential foundation of the system foredooms it to failure. Here we have a book which is believed by every Muslim without exception to be literally and actually the very words of God Himself, written in a language which is the language of heaven. If God speaks He would speak in Arabic (there are not a few Christians in England who think that God speaks English and belongs to the Church of England!), and hence the pride shown by the Ulema in the Holy Cities for their language. This book therefore is not only the true, final, and perfect revelation in all matters pertaining to man's eventual beatitude, but also lays down the law for every part of a Muslim's life. Where it appears to be uncertain or to contradict itself, as in many cases, the Sunnat or Traditions of the Prophet is there to elucidate the matter. We find, therefore, millions of our fellow-beings regulating their moral conduct, social life, and political activities by certain directions drawn up for a few Arab tribes 1,500 years ago. From such rules none may swerve by a hair's-breadth.

Islam imposes upon its followers an intellectual tyranny that is unbelievable to those who have not lived in its midst. It is an example of an extreme theocracy without God. It is utterly impossible for Muslim powers to keep abreast with the general advance of civilisation, for intellectually they are incapable of expansion. Originality of thought is sin. Speculation, within the limits laid down by the four legalists, is the utmost to which they can aspire.

A desire for learning and education, when gratified, produces the contemptuous agnosticism so prevalent among the Effendi class in Baghdad. Any attempt at social reform and improvements is impossible. In this connection, the Rev. Edward Sell refers to a meeting held by a number of Muslims at Poona in December 1895, to decide whether they should take part with Hindus in a conference to consider the question of social reforms. It was resolved not to do so on this ground: 'In the face of the Quran it is altogether needless for the Musulmans to join in any purely sectional conference, for Islam is a perfect exponent of social

THE SYSTEM

emancipation and human progress in all its aspects' (*Madras Weekly Mail*).

A suggestion for a school in one of the small towns in my charge met with the greatest opposition from the religious element, though in other parts of the country, further removed from the influence of the Holy Cities, schools had been welcomed. The representative of the Chief Mujtahid asked me to pay him a visit. He was furious at the idea. Had they not already a school – did not the children sit at the feet of the Mullah in the mosque every day? When I inquired about the curriculum, I was told that they learnt all that was necessary, verses of the Quran by heart, and sufficient knowledge of reading and writing. Fortunately I was in a position to say that this school was going to be closed down at once. The old gentleman was white with passion, but he had to give way. My immediate subordinate was a Muslim from Syria, though actually an atheist. He was therefore able to enter the mosque. In this particular case he had found that six children used to come for a couple of hours, four days a week, and that the mosque was also used as a public latrine! It appeared that this had been the custom for quite a long time, and it had not been cleansed for months. I was able therefore to inform the Holy Man that unless he himself ordered the closing of the school in the mosque, I should be compelled to inform the Chief Mujtahid for what other purpose the Bait Allah (the House of God) was being used. It was closed down that afternoon, and subsequently the Education Department opened a school in Najaf itself. The stagnation of the Shia' is well shown by the

THE INS AND OUTS OF MESOPOTAMIA

fact that in the teachers' training college at Baghdad, only five, out of about fifty, students were Shia', though the country is almost solely Shia', and Sunni masters are not allowed in the schools!

The effect of Islam on a people considered as a political unit is no less disastrous. The condition of Persia and the fate of those countries formerly within the Turkish Empire are sufficient to show this. The utter intolerance shown to anyone who attempts to institute a reform from within is well seen in the history of the Bab movement in Persia, which originated in Kerbela, of which full details can be found in the books of Professor Browne. Suffice it to say here, that those in sympathy with the movement were subjected to such persecutions and tortures as were previously unknown even in Persia, that land of Satanic cruelty. Infinitely greater fury and disgust are shown by his Co-religionists towards a Muslim who dares to speculate on his faith, than would be shown to a kafir. The Shia' of Najaf or Kerbela much prefers the Christian to the Sunni or the despised Sufi (Mystics), or the presumptuous Bab Bahai.[1] A Sufi who made his way into Najaf very nearly caused a riot, and lost his life into the bargain. His eventual escape was engineered by the Political Officer, who sent him off in a Ford car at two o'clock in the morning. The next day the coffee-shops were discussing one of the world-shaking utterances of the Chief Mujtahid, which was: 'The slaying of a Sufi

---

[1] He through whom, in the belief of this particular sect, the Hidden Imam speaks. *Bab* means the 'door'.

THE SYSTEM

is an act peculiarly well pleasing to God and His Prophet.'

The effect of the System of Islam, upon the 'believer', has been admirably summed up by Professor Smythe. The effects he enumerates have to be infinitely multiplied, when the Shia' is concerned. He says:

'Muhammad taught predestination, and his followers have thus become, by their crude application of his doctrine, the victims of every natural disease and calamity. He practised intolerance, and they are thus made the enemies of the civilised world. He permitted the union of the Legal and Sacerdotal Offices, and he made the book of his religion and his legislation the same. All alterations among the Muhammadan must have been thought impiety. Lost in the scale of thinking beings, they have exhibited families without society, subjects without freedom, Governments without security, and nations without improvement.'

Yet in spite of this hopeless system – a system which is as rigid as is possible to conceive, which admits of no originality, no progress, which is narrower than the narrowest Calvinism, which is intellectually and morally dead, and which holds its followers bound hand and foot to a legalism that kills all aspiration and strangles at birth every effort – in spite of all this, Islam is the great rival of Christianity, and in those parts of the world, e.g. Africa, where the two proselytise side by side, it is making headway against our own faith.

I propose to examine shortly the reasons for this phenomenon, for when the official religion of all

THE INS AND OUTS OF MESOPOTAMIA

the progressive nations is being supplanted by that of those peoples who are universally renowned for obscurantism, decadence, and political corruption, the matter becomes one of the most pressing political questions.

The soul-killing system of Islam is, from one point of view, its strength. It has acted on the individual and, through the individual, on the mass. Such terms as 'the unchanging East' are a criticism of Islamic influence. The number of Muslims in China is negligible, in Japan they are almost non-existent, and we find those countries daily advancing towards a realisation of national soul-consciousness. On the other hand, moving westwards to India, we see a vast upheaval in process, a strenuous bringing to birth of something – it may be a monster – but something, which is inflicting hideous pangs on the country. Now I do not believe for a moment that this is a desire for progress, as we understand it and as it is understood in Japan or China. It is rather the very opposite, a desire to be left alone.

The Hindu would fain revert to the ancient days of Hind with its Gurukuls, the training of its children in the old way (25 years a student, 25 a warrior, 25 a householder, and 25 a religious). The people are tired of the rush of competition, the hurry and bustle of the Western races, and sigh for a return to the placid life of bygone days. The Muslim looks back to the days of Akbar and the Mogul Empire. Neither party could effect anything single-handed, but the fraternising of the two great faiths has more and more tended to Islamise Hindu thought. And further westward, the same

THE SYSTEM

thing repeats itself, with greater intensity, as we draw near the centres of Islam, Constantinople, the seat of the Khaliph, and Mecca, the shrine of the Kaaba. The universal viewpoint is hopeless, happy-go-lucky and unidealistic, rendering effort of any kind as preposterous – to quote our American brothers – as 'a snowflake in hell!'

'Inshallah bukra' ('God willing, tomorrow') is the cry throughout Arabia. The individual will refuse to stir himself. He has no sense of cohesion or cooperation for the common good. He lives for himself alone, and is supremely content in the knowledge of his own superiority. Islam demands from the faithful no individual effort, and it is this fact which secures it the mission field.

The Muslim is excessively proud, and between Muslim and Muslim there is, in one sense, a real brotherhood. A body of Muslims meeting in a foreign country would be far more closely united than a body of Christians in the same circumstances. It must, indeed, be admitted that Islam is far preferable to Animism, and it is over this primitive and degraded faith that the Muslim missionary attains his chief power. He demands nothing from the convert save the recitation of a formula, and submission to the rite of circumcision, to which, however, most savage tribes have already submitted. He offers a membership of a huge society; he plays on the innate antagonism of colour against the white races; and he works for converts among those who, like himself, have no desire for progress and all the effort that progress implies. The Muslim missionary does not as a rule settle among his converts, but passes on, leaving his flock in precisely

THE INS AND OUTS OF MESOPOTAMIA

the same moral condition as of old. Only 'Muhammad' has replaced a tree or a stone. They are Muslims only in name, but, as members of this worldwide faith, they are conscious of a new sense of superiority, and that is enough! The converts are not sufficiently developed to appreciate the subtler virtues of unselfishness, truthfulness, and gentleness. They understand roughness, cruelty, drunkenness, fornication, lying, and theft. Here is an enormous weapon, wielded with much skill by the Muslim.

Our unique gifts for colonisation have placed upon us a responsibility far wider than we often trouble to realise. The mind of the heathen cannot possibly comprehend the difference between a Christian in name and in deed. To him all white men are Christian. He, in his heathen days, has been peculiarly careful to observe the necessary rites of his 'faith'. He has offered his sacrifices, he has obeyed the witch-doctor and paid him the proper fees, he has worn the right charms and seen that his children do the same. He may then come under the influence of a Christian missionary, and learn the obligations of the Christian faith.

If, however, he subsequently goes into the nearest town, he will not infrequently find that the white population, who are to his mind all Christian, do not pay any regard to such obligations. The effect of climate on the moral character is great, and, coupled with a slackening of the laws of convention so rigorous at home, frequently works havoc with the white man abroad. The in-

THE SYSTEM

consistency has been remarked over and over again by Muslims to our great detriment.

There is yet another problem we should not overlook. What accounts for the fact that a new convert to Islam always proves adamant in his newly adopted faith?

In the first place, the renegade would in all probability be murdered. But, more fundamentally, he has been, literally, captured by the system, and any kind of impulse towards self-improvement, once perhaps in his nature, has been effectually damped.

What are the alternatives?

Islam offers him an assurance of heaven, and an obviously attractive heaven at that: also the friendship of all Muslims wherever he may be. It demands from him no personal effort, for he is now a true believer, and the Prophet will intercede for him. He need not even pray – indeed, he will not be able to, for prayer is LAWFUL only in Arabic, which to him is an unknown tongue. Finally (and this has great influence), he has been given a definite sense of superiority over, and union against, the much-disliked white man. It is not unknown that the English in general, but more especially the commercial class, are most heartily disliked by the majority of the indigenous peoples abroad.

On the other hand, Christianity only offers an assurance of heaven IF CERTAIN LAWS ARE KEPT. This will compel him to forsake the habits which have been handed down in his community since the beginning of time, and involve a perpetual self-discipline. It will mean a constant sense of discomfort, from the birth of a sense of sin – a perpetual warfare in his consciousness. In many cases, it must bring not the sense of companionship and union, but a very practical experience of persecution and contempt. And what is the end and aim of so much unaccustomed effort? It is loyalty and devotion to a Personality, who has so little hold on those who are born Christians that their public actions, to be seen of all men, too often betray what the convert knows to be deliberate disobedience to His commands.

It is, finally, essential for us to understand the power of Islam in Muslim lands. No doubt it may be partly explained by the low standard it demands from the faithful. I do not, of course, refer to the actual teaching of the Quran. Were the standard of morality therein laid down strictly observed, there would be little ground for complaint. But as the vast majority of Muslims are utterly ignorant of their Holy Book, we cannot judge them by it. The power of Islam depends, in my opinion, on two things:

(1) The ignorance of the people, and the consequent tyranny of the Religious Hierarchy.

(2) The power of *personalities* (over the orthodox, of Muhammad, and over the Shia' of Ali, Hussein, and the Prophet).

The first point is indeed obvious to all. The Shia' of Iraq is absolutely certain – as certain as he can be of anything in the world – that the word of the Chief Mujtahid can plunge him into everlasting damnation; so desirable a belief is naturally encouraged by the Ulema.

The second reason, however, will bear some examination, and is, moreover, the main foundation

THE SYSTEM

on which the psychology of the people has been developed. There is a consciousness in each individual of a personal relationship between himself and Ali or Hussein. The anger of Allah is nothing, compared to the anger of Hussein. Many and many a man will take the oath 'Wallahi wa billahi wa tillahi' ('By God and in God and through God') in the law courts – while the Quran, wrapped in a dirty duster (lest it be defiled by the hand of the witness), is laid upon his eyes – and will yet immediately commit the most gross and deliberate perjury. Not one, however, would lie after taking an oath on the Shrine of Ali at Najaf, or of Hussein or Abbas at Kerbela. In ordinary conversation, a sentence which commences with 'Wallah!' is quite likely to be a deliberate falsehood; but should it begin with 'Wa l'Nabi', or 'wa Abbas', i.e. 'By the Prophet', or 'By Abbas', you may be almost sure of hearing the truth. In foul or abusive language the Arab, particularly in the towns, is unique. His obscenity will pass all the bounds of imagination; but you will never hear the name of the Prophet or the Saints of Islam in conjunction with such phrases. I never met with real devotion, such as we understand it, save at the time of Muharram, in honour of Hussein. That devotion was shared by man and woman, rich and poor alike.

The question of oaths in general may be considered at this point, for it will be generally admitted that the building-up of a stable form of government rests finally on the integrity of the individual. Islam has quite definitely assumed the responsibility for a theory which strikes at the very basis of all social development. It has defi-

THE INS AND OUTS OF MESOPOTAMIA

nitely and unequivocally given official sanction to the breaking of oaths. This is not an abuse which has grown up through a misunderstanding of Quranic teaching, as in the case of promiscuous divorce, but a clearly authorised practice. Sura v. verse 89 reads:

'Allah does not call you to account for what is vain in your oaths, but He calls you to account for the making of deliberate oaths: so its expiation is the feeding of ten poor men out of the food you feed your families with, or their clothing or the freeing of a neck; but whoever cannot find means, then fasting for three days; this is the expiation of your oaths when you swear; and guard your oaths. Thus does Allah make clear to you His communications, that you may be grateful.'

In Sura lxvi. verse 2 we find:

'Allah has sanctioned for you the expiation of your oaths, but Allah is your protector and He is the Knowing, the Wise.'

The 'expiation of an oath' can only mean that perjury may be atoned for by the performance of certain actions, and this teaching has been naturally so expanded that any 'good' deed will now suffice. And this is by no means a modern development of Islam. It has been the ordinary practice ever since its foundation. Professor Margoliouth cites two well-known instances, which I quote. They could of course be multiplied a thousandfold.

THE SYSTEM

'Dangerous consequences were drawn from the Prophet's doctrine, emphasised on the occasion of a domestic irregularity, that an oath might be cancelled by some substituted performance. According to the Tradition, one of the Companions of the Prophet, Zubair, who had started the revolt against Ali, was persuaded by the latter to abandon his project and gave what seemed a solemn oath that he would not take part in a war against the Khaliph. Zubair's son, who afterwards endeavoured to maintain himself as sovereign, persuaded his father to make atonement for his oath by freeing a slave, and to take his place in the battlefield as if nothing had happened.

'The unscrupulous adventurer Mukhtar who, by posing as the avenger of Hussein, shed blood in rivers, had been imprisoned by the Governor in Kufa, when some suspicion of his plans leaked out. Owing to the intercession of Omar's highly respected son, the Governor was persuaded to give Mukhtar his liberty, but not before making him take the most solemn oaths that he would not head an insurrection. Mukhtar, we are told, readily took the oaths offered, thinking to himself what a fool the Governor of Kufa must be to suppose an oath could make any difference when it was so easy to substitute some other performance for it; particularly as it might easily be maintained that taking vengeance for the death of Hussein was a duty which took precedence over all others. Like Zubair, then, Mukhtar perjured himself without scruple.

'Yet in perjuring themselves they had the authority of the Quran behind them, and were acting well within the Law. The oath of a Muslim sovereign or commander was worth nothing at all, though public opinion seems sometimes to have been moved by very flagrant violations.'[1]

1 *Early Development of Muhammadanism.*

THE INS AND OUTS OF MESOPOTAMIA

The result of such teachings is seen everywhere and in every walk of life; but more especially among the Ruasa, or leaders of society, both religious and secular. Pointless lying is the rule – so much so that it has become a normal habit – almost an unconscious mental impulse.

A certain Sheikh Abdul Wahad, a notorious seditionist and exceptionally pious according to Islamic standard, came to visit me in connection with a piece of land which he and his younger brother both claimed. The land lay between their respective properties, and, naturally, each had his own version of the facts. Unfortunately for them, neither knew that I happened to have in my possession a document in which the sale of this land, and all particulars of its rightful ownership were recorded in due form. The actual owner, in fact, had been deported to India and had died. His heirs had fled at the time and, being poor folk, were entirely without influence. Here, it had seemed, was a magnificent chance for the robber-barons to fulfil their vocation. They had banked on the practical certainty that the owner had taken the document away with him, and that it was now irretrievably lost. And here is the point. The receipt actually bore the signature and seal of the two brothers, who had witnessed the transaction in the 'madhif' of Abdul Wahad!!

When confronted with it, however, neither showed the least embarrassment. I turned to the elder.

'Why is your honour such an infernal liar?' I asked. He replied, 'Oh, it is our habit. I lie to my brother and he to me when it is convenient. It is

THE SYSTEM

our way, is it not, Hassan?' The other laughingly acknowledged that indeed that was so.

Apart altogether from the soul-killing religious system of Islam described above, this latter characteristic would be sufficient to ensure the collapse of any Muslim nation. It cuts away the very foundation of all society, and must effectually prevent the growth of national consciousness or political unity. The abomination of 'taqiya',[1] which is peculiar to the Shia', adds a deadly force to this conclusion.

We must, however, endeavour to understand the sanctity that *does* belong to an asseveration, in the names of Ali, Hussein, or Abbas. To account for this, it is necessary to grasp the type of character for which the Prophet legislated, and the ideal he desired to enforce by that legislation. Primarily, and above everything else, his adherents were fighters – and he was clever enough to see that any new 'faith' which did not put war first, would entirely fail to secure any adherents. It was a stroke of genius to disguise the Arab raid (their chief form of amusement) as a defence of the faith, while the revelation of assured salvation and instantaneous passage to a most desirable heaven for those who died fighting increased the efficiency of his army a thousandfold.

The most devout Muslim was the bravest fighter, and conversely. Here was a teaching that every Arab could understand, and which has stamped Islam for ever as the religion which de-

[1] Meaning that it is the *duty* of a Shia' to break faith with and deceive the unbeliever, as explained in Chapter V.

THE INS AND OUTS OF MESOPOTAMIA

pends for its existence on force. For his immediate purpose, nothing could have been more subtly devised. The Saints of Islam, therefore, are those who excelled in the battlefield, and here none have surpassed Ali and his sons. To Ali alone was given the name of the Lion, and on the walls of the houses in Najaf, both within and without, we often see this emblem of the first Imam. Amazing legends are still told round the fire in the 'madhifs' of the tribes, about the skill, strength, and bravery in warfare of the three heroes. Ali is represented as an immense figure, whose spear no five Muslims could lift. Hussein slew with his own hand two thousand of those who attacked him in the Battle of Kerbela, and he only eventually died because he *allowed the enemy to slay him*.

There can be no doubt that, in the days of the Prophet and immediately after, there was a virility in Islam which is conspicuous by its absence in these days. The reason is obvious. The circumstances which produced the characteristic spirit of Islam are changed. They have no opportunities for further conquest, and nothing is left but an empty shell of legalism and hair-splitting. Thus the *official* teaching no longer makes any appeal to the masses. They live and thrive on the memory of their saints, whose moral qualities are rarely if ever remembered, but whose feats in the battlefield form an unfailing source of conversation. What use has the cultivator for Allah? None. That Allah may be the Merciful, the Wise, the Judge to the ninety-ninth power,[1] is of absolutely no inter-

---

[1] In Islam there are ninety-nine titles applied to Allah.

est to him, and has no effect on his daily life. But the stature of Ali or Hussein, the way they fought, the blows they gave, the slaughter which they themselves carried out single-handed, the streams of blood which marked their passage through the hordes of the enemy, these are things that the people understand. Here are natural human personalities, exhibiting the perfection of the very qualities that they themselves possess: physical endurance and bravery in warfare; a love of bloodshed, cruelty, and oppression; a steadfastness and patience in suffering, which is characteristic of all the tribesmen.

In the light of the foregoing pages, it is interesting to speculate on the mentality of those who desire to see 'national aspirations gratified' and talk learnedly about the 'unity of the Arab race'.

About the time of the Peace Conference there appears to have been a wave of emotional enthusiasm in many to whom the Arab and Islam were a closed book; and also in some who ought to have known better. After all, politicians who dwell in Whitehall cannot be expected to refuse advice from those whom they believe to be experts; and if those experts give way to an orgy of sentimentality – well, it is a periodic failing of the Anglo-Saxon, and, as we have learnt many times over, very apt to prove expensive.

There is no unity of the Arab race, as Western democracies understand the term. If it be said that there *was* a very definite demand for an Amir of the House of Hussein of Mecca in Mesopotamia, I reply that the wish was father to the thought, as will appear from my next chapter.

THE INS AND OUTS OF MESOPOTAMIA

What is the 'Arab race'? Does it include everyone who dwells in Arabia and Mesopotamia, with the communities of indigenous Christians, whose existence seems to have been entirely overlooked? Or does it mean only those inhabitants who are indeed all Muslims, but of divided faith: the Sunni, the Shia', and the Wahabi? Can a community unite who are divided from each other by the most impassable gulf known to history – religious feuds and hatred? In Mesopotamia, at any rate, these 'national aspirations' mean no more than a demand from a few irresponsible robber-barons, who know that self-government will mean an enormous increase in their own liberty to rob and extort, with a complete exemption from the payment of revenue. 'It is a hard fact that to the local taxpayer a native Government means nothing except remission of all taxes; for he at least is not credulous of the ability of a native Government to collect these.'[1]

These catch-phrases, however, were very useful to us in disguising the fact that we were FORCED to follow a certain line of action in Mesopotamia and Palestine. I cannot believe that those responsible for our present policy were ignorant of the condition of affairs in Islam in general, and particularly among the Arabs. That self-government for these peoples may be possible, say, one hundred years hence, is perhaps true; but to suggest such a thing at the present time is the veriest eyewash and camouflage. The real reasons which

---

[1] *An Administrator in the Making*, by J. S. Mann.

THE SYSTEM

lie at the back of the present *affaire* of the Middle East, I hope to outline in the following pages.

PART II

POLITICAL SITUATION AND THE FUTURE

CHAPTER I

ENGLAND AND MESOPOTAMIA

Past record of Islam. The Anglo-French Declaration. At the Peace Conference. Effect of war *against* Turkey. Appeal to Mecca. The 'Terms'. Muslim intrigues. The Interregnum in Mesopotamia. The revolution. Sir Arnold Wilson and firmness. Sir Percy Scott and the 'Constitution'. Feisal and inefficiency.

THE BRITISH EMPIRE, the greatest Christian Empire the world has ever seen, may well be called the foster-mother of Islam. Millions of our subjects owe allegiance to the Prophet Muhammad, and jointly regulate their conduct by that astounding book, the Quran, and *by laws laid down for them by their Christian rulers*. It is to be noted that such laws are the outcome of a social consciousness directly traceable to Christian influence. Individual members of the British executive may confess themselves to be atheist or agnostic, but the Laws and the justice they administer are the direct outcome of the community-life with which the Early Church was saturated. Had it not been for the new social and intellectual obligations imposed upon it from without by a Christian Power, it is not inconceivable that, however popular as a domestic faith, Islam would have died long since of inanition. Almost certainly, it would not now have to be reckoned with as a world force. It has been bolstered up and rendered strong by institutions utterly foreign to its own spirit.

For what is the history of this religion, which its adherents claim to be 'a perfect exponent of social emancipation and human progress in all its aspects', and which should therefore be judged by its effects on the culture and progress of society in general?

Is it not one long record of failure? It has everywhere deadened all aspiration and all desire for self-improvement. There have been periods of great brilliancy in Islamic history, fertile in intellect and culture; periods which stand out all the more vividly in contrast to the dingy background. It is, however, significant that they have always coincided with the ascendancy of the heterodox. No one would question the genius shown by Akbar and his so-called Muslim administration. But Akbar was a noted heretic. He was a true ruler, in the best and most literal sense of the term, who openly declared that there was truth in all faiths, that each man was endeavouring to find God in his own way, and that all were to be encouraged along their own lines. He filled his Court with men of similar mentality, and extended his patronage to the philosophers and doctors of all creeds. If Orthodox Islam takes credit for his rule, it must acknowledge the progressive outlook of the heretic! During Islamic domination in Spain, on the other hand, all speculation in higher matters of thought was rigidly suppressed. On the expulsion of the

ENGLAND AND MESOPOTAMIA

Moors, they sank back into that condition of torpidity so symptomatic of Muslim character.

Persia is an excellent example of a Muslim despotism, almost unaffected by Western influence. It is a byword for misgovernment, bribery, cruelty, and unnameable vice. It has been touched by the clammy hand of political death and the other, even worse, hand of Shia' Islam.

In Mesopotamia itself the country has been reduced from a state of world-famous productivity and fruitfulness to a sterility which was accurately described by a British Tommy as 'miles and miles and miles of damn-all'. There are, it is true, still tracts of land of marvellous beauty and fertility; but as a whole it can only be regarded as a desert, and the blight of the land has fallen on the inhabitants thereof. Its past history is one of perpetual feuds and bloodshed. Sect after sect arose, venting their fury against one another by murder and massacre. Now and again, periods of comparative peace would arise, such as that under the first three Abbaside Khaliphs (who lent all their support to the Muta'zilahs, or free-thinkers, and persecuted the orthodox with the greatest vigour). During this period, when men were allowed full scope to their intelligence and the speculative impulse of the human brain, we catch glimpses of the brilliance of the Arab mentality. But tyranny and treachery soon brought back the orthodox into power.

Ever since the country passed from the hands of the Persian Empire into those of Islam, it has always needed the strongest and most severe Gover-

THE INS AND OUTS OF MESOPOTAMIA

nors, since none of weaker calibre could cope with its peoples.

'The broad fact to be accounted for is the general decadence of the Muhammadan world. To whichever quarter we look – to North Africa, Egypt, Arabia, the Ottoman Empire, Persia – the same spectacle of decay and increasing decrepitude confronts us. It cannot be urged that Islam is not responsible for this state of things on the ground that Islam is merely a religion and not a system of government. Islam is both. Neither can it be urged in defence of Islam that this or that country has enjoyed transient periods of greatness or prosperity, notwithstanding its dominating presence. The very fact that these periods have left no lasting memorials behind them, in the shape of improved laws or civic freedom, furnishes the strongest proof that reform and growth are utterly alien to the enduring spirit of Islam.'

This is abundantly true of all Muslim realms, and peculiarly so of the 'land of the two rivers', which from time immemorial has been an undying furnace of intrigue and rebellion, of treachery and murder, defying all law and order.

'It has been the storm-centre of South-West Asia, from which the majority of the great religious schisms and disruptions arose. Even in the days of Ali, it produced the Khawarij, whose main principle was to oppose the established order of belief and society, and to clamour for a theocracy, by which they really meant anarchy and nihilism.'

ENGLAND AND MESOPOTAMIA

This is exactly what is occurring at the present time. That the Arabs of Mesopotamia 'don't want us' is nothing new. They have never wanted anyone or any form of government which could restrain their inherited instinct for lawlessness and violent crime. They are now crying out to a sentimental Europe, pleading for the right to express the soul-consciousness of the 'Arab nation', bolstered up by English sentimentalists who ought to know better. This means the old dream, by a new path.

No doubt, many will answer: 'If that is so, then let them have it.' Unfortunately, the consequences would prove impossible – for the world!

The administrative inefficiency and ineptitude of Islamic peoples throughout history, and the turbulent, anarchical character of the inhabitants of Mesopotamia, are perfectly well known to those European statesmen who are versed in matters affecting the Near and Middle East. That it should be otherwise is incredible. Persia affords a good example of what a Shia' Government really means, and offers a parallel to what might be expected from a self-governing Mesopotamia. It can hardly be urged that we were ignorant of conditions in that country, in face of the valuable information which the late Colonel Leachman, Major Soane, and Miss Gertrude Bell have given us about the tribes they travelled among and knew so well.

The Holy Cities of Najaf and Kerbela were, however, more or less of a closed book, though it is not possible that their influence can have been overlooked.

THE INS AND OUTS OF MESOPOTAMIA

Yet in spite of the knowledge that was in our hands, and our experience, as the greatest Muslim Power, of Islam's complete failure to govern itself or others, we have produced the Anglo-French Declaration!

This remarkable document, of which the full text will be found in the Appendix, was a declaration that we and the French wished all those countries in the Middle East which had been delivered from tyranny and misgovernment, to understand that they were now at liberty to express their own opinion as to what form of government they might desire in the future. It offered them the full opportunity of giving expression to their national consciousness and aspirations.

This political bombshell arrived one morning in Baghdad, as I well remember. I happened to be passing through the city on my way to Shamiyah, and, having some business in the Cypher Section, I went up there before breakfast. With the exception of the Cypher clerk, I believe I was the first person to read the document, with its startling order for immediate publication. I cannot believe that it was originally intended as anything more than sentimental eyewash, an appeal to a Europe revelling in the emotional reaction produced by the war. Incidentally, it would effectually limit the activities of the two signatory rival Powers in the areas named. Possibly, each regarded it as a useful temporary measure, to control the other, while they themselves got on with more important work, and until they could give greater attention to their mutual interests and adjustments in the Middle East.

ENGLAND AND MESOPOTAMIA

It has been recorded that, at the Versailles Peace Conference, the possibility of self-government for Mesopotamia was being discussed. Three *very* high politicians from Whitehall are said to have made the following remarks:

1st Politician. 'I fear that the country may be badly governed.'

2nd Politician. 'The country *will* be badly governed.'

3rd Politician. 'The country ought to be badly governed.'

This bears out my contention that our *beaux sabreurs* were perfectly well aware of what self-government in Mesopotamia must produce.

It is, in my opinion, a truism that the British Empire has never taken any 'interest' in a country from motives of 'pure philanthropy'. Why, indeed, should it? The Empire is a business concern first and foremost, and, by this standard, it has fully justified itself in whatever parts of the world it has absorbed. But the benefit has always been mutual. The universal outcry against our policy in Mesopotamia proves that the general public fully realise this. For the first time in our history we appear to be acting the part, not only of philanthropists, but of philanthropists full of folly.

To realise what led up to this astounding move, and what its effects actually have been and must prove to be, it is necessary to recall the whole trend of events in Mesopotamia – and in Islam – since the beginning of the war.

Mesopotamia cannot be regarded as an isolated unit. It is only one part of the lesser problem of the Arab peoples, and the greater problem of Islam.

THE INS AND OUTS OF MESOPOTAMIA

Our present policy must be referred back to the days when Turkey came into the war against us. As the great foster-mother of Islam we have always retained the diplomatic friendship of Turkey, whose ruler is the Khaliph (or Pontiff) of Orthodox Islam. The importance of such an alliance to our hold on our Muslim subjects of India, cannot be over-estimated; but till lately it has never been appreciated by those who have lived at home all their lives. To the orthodox believer, the Khaliph represents the whole of Islam in his own person. The shock, therefore, to the sensibilities of the Muslims in India when he declared war against us must have been shattering. The immediate necessity was to discover some means to counteract or at least mitigate the effect.

If the person of the Khaliph, by virtue of his office, is sacred, no less sacred are the cities of Mecca and Medina, the former containing the Kaaba (or most holy temple), and the latter the tomb, of the Prophet. The guardianship of the Kaaba has always been vested in one family (the Shariffs of Mecca), which is now represented by Hussein, who, from this position, wields considerable influence among the faithful.

The action of Turkey completely changed the whole outlook, which, up to that moment, had always secured for us at least the friendly disposition of all Muslims. A return to the *status quo ante* was quite impossible during the war, but the situation could at least be considerably improved by setting up Mecca in opposition to Constantinople. There was, however, an obvious risk in this policy of offending Islam, because the Sultan was not only the spiritual but also the temporal Chief of the Shariff.

Nevertheless it was adopted; and the conduct of Hussein, at this crisis, fully confirms my interpretation of the Arab character, proving also the want of understanding in those who talked – and still talk – about the 'noble Arab'. Negotiations, however, were in fact conducted by those who knew. There is only one way by which to obtain anything substantial from an Arab – and that is hard cash. The policy which followed has been associated with the name of Colonel Lawrence.

Lawrence was the accredited purse-bearer of the British Treasury to Hussein, Shariff of Mecca. The wealth of our Empire is well known throughout the East, and so soon as his mission was thoroughly understood, he was naturally welcomed with open arms.

Hussein, under the circumstances, was in a position to demand his own terms, and his natural aptitude for the part was quickly in evidence. So vitally necessary was his support, that it was tentatively suggested he should himself become Supreme Khaliph of All Islam. Now this suggestion was about as absurd as it would be for some Buddhist Power to propose inviting the Patriarch of Eastern Christendom to reign in the Vatican after dethroning the actual Pope!

Hussein coyly and courteously declined the proposed honour; but it served to show him how far we were prepared to go for his support. And he named his terms. These were what could naturally be expected from any member of the Religious Hierarchy of Islam – hard cash and power.

THE INS AND OUTS OF MESOPOTAMIA

Being practically bound to accept, we, the greatest Christian Empire, recognised the Shariff of Mecca as a king in his own land! (What must the Prophet think!) We found the cash to help him keep up his kingly estate; and paid him £5,000 a month.

For every reason, his kingdom must be at peace, and we therefore paid a further monthly subsidy of, I believe, £2,000, by way of a bribe to his neighbour and hereditary enemy, Ibn Saud, Sheikh of the Wahabis.

Then, finally, we found kingdoms for his two sons, Feisal and Abdullah.[1]

The venerable gentleman certainly exacted his pound of flesh, and it is difficult to think of anything else that he might have asked, and did not!

As we were then placed, by the inclusion of Turkey among our enemies – since, at all costs, the war had to be won and our Empire maintained intact – it is difficult to see what other policy we could have adopted. It is perhaps not impossible that cheaper 'terms' might have been obtained, but in such matters the Arab is a wily bird. Its immediate effect, at any rate, was noticeably to our advantage, through a definite steadying of Indian Muslim thought. Persia, being all Shia', and loathing the Sunni, was delighted to see the breakaway of Mecca from Constantinople, while, for the same reason, the tribes of Mesopotamia and the influence of the Holy Cities were at any rate not ac-

---

[1] The subsidy to the Shariff has lately been discontinued, but the original subsidy to Ibn Saud, of, I believe, £2,000 a month, has been increased to £5,000 a month. Cf. *The Times Parliamentary Report*, Nov. 29, 1922.

ENGLAND AND MESOPOTAMIA

tively against us. The benefit to the troops on our extended lines of communication can hardly be realised. The influence of the Shariff being paramount over the tribes of the Hedjaz, our right flank in the Palestine advance was not only secure, but supported by active help, while Muslim opinion in Egypt became no longer definitely anti-British.

In fact, all went well until the time came for the fulfilling of the promises. Cash had been literally ladled out, and kingdoms promised. The former concerned only ourselves, but the latter terms involved other Powers, in particular the French. The end of the war saw Feisal (son of Hussein) established by us as King of Syria and neighbour to the French, who, however, finding him quite impossible at close quarters, simply threw him out. He had to go, and go he did – to Downing Street, accompanied by his patron and sponsor, Colonel Lawrence. We all remember those days, when the public Press expatiated on the noble Arab *ad nauseam*. We remember our indignation at the way in which the French had treated our noble 'ally', but we did not foresee what that noble ally was going to cost us, each and individually, for maintaining him upon his throne, when found – as it eventually was, in Mesopotamia!

Some time before the crash came in Syria, it had been evident that Feisal and the French were two incompatibles, and, if we were to deliver the pound of flesh, another throne must be found. The part of Mesopotamia most amenable to influence from Mecca is the Shamiyah, wherein stands Najaf. Geographically it is the nearest, and in the meantime, originally without our knowledge, the Sheikhs themselves had been intriguing with Hussein to the same effect, though, of course, with the ultimate purpose of independence.

The policy of the Ottoman Government in Iraq had been to replace the powerful tribal confederacies by a number of large landed proprietors, Sheikhs, or Syeds, who enjoyed almost complete local autonomy, and preyed at will upon weaker and less fortunate neighbours. They regarded, with only too well-justified contempt, the feeble attempts of corrupt officials to collect 1 per cent of the revenue demand. The rapidly increasing prosperity of the Shamiyah, its distance from Baghdad and the proximity of Najaf – always a centre of intrigue and rebellion – all contributed towards a feeling of independence and confidence in their own abilities, which made the Shamiyah Sheikhs both the terror and despair of the Ottoman Government. Any effort towards collecting the revenue was invariably the prelude to quite extensive autumn manoeuvres on the part of several battalions, and the murder of the hated Sunni official was an agreeable pastime. At the outbreak of war in Mesopotamia, the Sheikhs of the Lower and Middle Euphrates sat on the fence with their usual skill, until the defeat of the Turk at the Battle of Shaiba – and then bundled him out neck and crop.

During the ensuing year our forces were far too occupied in driving the Turk out of the country to attempt to establish an efficient Civil Administration of the Shamiyah, the most cultivated and the most turbulent province of a turbulent country. A

ENGLAND AND MESOPOTAMIA

sort of interregnum occurred there, during which the Sheikhs developed to the full their inherent talents for the parts of robber-barons and marauders.

Needless to say, this period did NOT involve the detestable obligation to pay revenue!

It was not until 1917 that this part of the country could be dealt with. For the first time in the memory of man the Sheikhs found themselves subjected to discipline; that is, an ordered Government and the payment of revenue, the latter in particular being a phenomenon which hit all the harder by contrast with the lawless interregnum which had just come to an end. That the revolution of 1920 was delayed so long was due entirely and solely to the untiring efforts of Sir Arnold Wilson, the head of the Civil Administration.

Though the Turkish revenue *demand* was, in some cases, as high as 60 per cent, the great Sheikhs rarely paid more than a fraction, the very greatest nothing at all! Our demand varied from 36 per cent to 33 per cent, but we actually secured about 25 per cent. It was inevitable that resentment should begin to crystallise and express itself in vague burblings, but it had not become definitely anti-British until the bombshell of the Anglo-French Declaration! This involved a definite inquiry, by local Political Officers, of the Sheikhs and other Ruasa (or leaders), as to their desires for the future of the country. Conceive the situation. Those who had spent the whole of their lives under an age-long tradition of rebellion against all and any sort of government, were now asked their opinion as to what sort of government they would choose.

But 'orders is orders', and they were obeyed!

The Sheikhs, while continuing their own intrigues with Mecca, were, of course, perfectly aware of British negotiations in the same quarter. To them it would seem that, if these all-conquering holders of India had been forced to seek assistance from a creature they knew they could use for their own ends, they might surely turn us out, as they had driven away the Turks.

Under a nominal Amir from the house of the Shariff, they could do what they liked. Returning to the happy period of the interregnum, there would be no revenue to pay, no law, and no justice – save what each Sheikh or Syed, or Mujtahid might choose to wield for his own advantage. Should the Amir attempt anything beyond nominal control, the slogan of 'Sunni' (the hated orthodox) could be raised to silence his pretensions.

I remember that when, subsequently, I tackled the very pious Abdul Wahad on his apostasy in having desired a Sunni ruler, he positively blushed, and, in his confusion, replied, 'They say he is Shia' at heart!'

At the same time Baghdad itself was in a ferment. An infamous old gentleman of the Suwaidi family was the arch-plotter – infamous, because he so persistently asseverated his undying friendship for the British – but not more infamous than the average Muslim intriguer with a reputation for 'holiness'. Plot and counter-plot went on apace. Messengers from Baghdad and from the tribes were sent to Feisal and his entourage in Syria

ENGLAND AND MESOPOTAMIA

with hair-raising stories of the wicked and appalling tyranny that was imposed upon them by the abominable despotism of Sir Arnold Wilson and the members of his Administration. That sort of charge must be expected from the Oriental, but it was surprising to find that British Officers, presumably well acquainted with his little ways, not only pretended to believe such stories, but deeply sympathised with the 'victims'.

Sir Arnold Wilson was in a most intolerable position. The Anglo-French Declaration had inspired the leaders of the people with hopes far beyond their own wildest dreams. They had been further encouraged by the inquiry into their own ideas of what government they desired. And then nothing happened, for the Civil Commissioner was not yet permitted to make that definite announcement of future policy which would have worked wonders and saved many lives.

The idea grew that to inquire, or consult them, did not pledge us to any consideration of their opinions. They were to be baulked of their glorious future. Then came the expulsion of Feisal from Syria *by our allies* and, presumably, with our consent, if not approval. It was now clear that, having obtained all we could from Mecca, we were ready deliberately to break faith with Hussein. There was no further hope for the future in Mesopotamia.

Out with the British tyrants. The revolution burst upon us. Baghdad, indeed, made no move, but the tribes rose as they had promised Shamiyah.

THE INS AND OUTS OF MESOPOTAMIA

If there was any man more than another who deserved the whole-hearted support of his countrymen at this time, it was Sir Arnold Wilson. Yet he was let down again and again. Maligned by those in England, even by those who had formerly worked under him (even by one or two actually supposed to be working loyally *with him* in Baghdad at the time), he cheerfully accepted complete responsibility and reduced the country to order once more. The chief Arab agitators and the leaders of risings among the tribes were sentenced to deportation, since, under the guise of friendship, they had planned and attempted the murders of British Officers and men.

The situation had been greatly complicated by Bolshevist propaganda throughout Persia, which permeated into the country via Persian pilgrims to the Holy Cities. The Turkish general Mustapha Kemal was agitating in the north; ex-Turkish employees, and hangers-on of the Shariffian house, began to drift in, and added yet another flavour to the already unholy brew.

Sir Percy Cox now arrived in Baghdad, where all this turmoil was slowly settling down. His coming had been widely advertised, and he was regarded by the Arab inhabitants as the harbinger of peace and good-will – good-will meaning in their eyes an immediate 'istiqlal', or independence. He was accompanied by Mr. Philby and Mr. Garbett, both of the Indian Civil, the former well known for his journeys across Central Arabia to Riadh, the headquarters of the Wahabi sect, under Ibn Saud. He brought with him that declaration of policy that had been so long awaited, and which, had it been made earlier, would almost certainly have averted the actual tragedy of revolution. Even now, made by one who had already such a tremendous reputation among the Arabs, it had an immediate effect, and great hopes were expressed for the new regime which had started under such auspicious circumstances.

It was unfortunate that the local feeling against Sir Arnold Wilson's Administration was encouraged by the new staff. One of its first acts was the recall of the infamous Suwaidi by telegram (or so his son informed me!). Others punished by Wilson were now pardoned, while those who had fled, fearing the wrath to come, were invited to return. Revenue was remitted on all sides, and the Arabs were loud in their praise of this most excellent Government. The enormous remission of revenue, in particular to just those Sheikhs who had been the leaders of the revolution, was bound eventually to react on the taxpayer at home and no sound reason for such a policy has been advanced. Of course political headquarters in Baghdad were simply bubbling over with 'legitimate aspirations', 'cultural genius', and the 'national consciousness of the Arab race'. There were a few who really seemed to think that they were fulfilling the part of saviour from the 'bigoted tyranny' of Wilson. No doubt some temporary reaction was inevitable, and it would have done no great harm as an indication of a forgiving policy, but one or two ill-balanced enthusiasts were so reckless as to criticise Sir Arnold before the local Baghdadi, without a moment's consideration of the effect on Oriental minds.

THE INS AND OUTS OF MESOPOTAMIA

A proper constitution was now promised, with a Legislative Assembly, to be elected by ballot. The scheme for election, however, was never promulgated, and the election never held, for the Cairo Conference was suddenly summoned. Our real object was to establish, in consultation with the Sheikhs, a final and permanent form of administration, the prospect of self-government being maintained by the appointment of ex-Turkish officials and friends of Feisal to posts formerly held by British Officers. Since Feisal was now without either a kingdom or a throne, it would have been dangerous to risk the uncertainties of an election. Meanwhile, Baghdad became more and more populated with the Feisal entourage – hangers-on – who had hoped for great things from the Syrian Court, and now rushed into Baghdad to secure some post or other in the future kingdom. Among others was the somewhat striking personality of Jaafar Pasha, the 'Commander-in-Chief' of the Arab army yet to be! A tall, corpulent figure, he had fought for the Turks, been taken prisoner, joined our forces, and was thereupon given the C.M.G. The title of 'Pasha' was literally self-made; but he was a genial soul and an excellent raconteur.

The Ministry of the Interior was given to Syed Talib Pasha – a gentleman whose reputation was about as gory as that of anyone east of Suez, but who was really a strong man, terribly feared by all and sundry. His record may well have been exaggerated – 'give a dog a bad name and hang him', and there is no question that, through his efforts on behalf of the British during the revolution, he saved many lives. He was subsequently deported; probably because a man of such immense ambition would not have endured Feisal for a moment. He was sacrificed for our debt to Mecca, but he carried with him the very real gratitude of not a few.

The Ministry of Education went to a Persian, from the Holy City of Kerbela, who, in an Arabic-speaking country, could neither read nor write Arabic. He has since been replaced. For the Ministry of Justice, the Chief Mufti of Mecca was brought over.

This looked very well on paper, and no doubt it edified the European Press, but a more hopelessly inefficient crew could hardly be imagined. With the exception of Syed Talib, and Sassoon Effendi – a most capable Jew in charge of Finance – there was not a competent man among them all.

Finally, Feisal himself (aptly termed the 'jack-in-the-box' king) came up the river, accompanied by an arch-rebel or two. He was duly enthroned as Amir of Iraq, *without* the issue of a single voting-paper, as it was now entirely certain that, except by the tribes of the Middle Euphrates, he was nowhere wanted. But the debt had to be paid!

To such an extent was 'Feisal' propaganda carried on before his arrival, that one or two Sheikhs were under the impression that he was Shia'! Now, it is necessary to establish in the country a strong garrison of British troops in order to keep a Sunni Amir over a Shia' people. It is all undoubtedly very amusing and Gilbertian, but hardly satisfactory to the taxpayer. We are told that this garrison can be recalled when 'King' Feisal has his Arab army. The recruiting, however, has not so far proceeded with the enthusiasm that was hoped, and the vision of a Sunni with a Shia' bodyguard must be reserved for the 'Day of Requital'!

I hope it is now clear that, for at least one urgent reason, we must stay in Iraq. Our hostility to Constantinople has already produced infinite trouble in India. The policy of attaching Mecca to our side during the war has to a certain extent discountenanced this natural feeling of antagonism. But Feisal certainly could not hold the throne of Iraq for one week without the support of our troops. If we left we should thus have quite definitely broken faith, and the enmity of Mecca (with all that it implies) would be an additional weight in the scales against us.

Is it worth the risk? The cry of 'oil-fields in Persia' is beside the mark. It is obvious that such concerns, which are international, could be easily protected by far less costly means.

Though, as an isolated policy, our presence in Mesopotamia seems to involve a criminal and wanton extravagance, it surely falls into perspective, and justifies itself as part of the immense Problem of Empire. As the key to the future of our dominions, it will appear less futile and less fatuous to the 'man in the street', who, whatever else he may be, is an Imperialist at heart.

CHAPTER II

THE FUTURE

Complete, or partial evacuation. Ibn Saud and the Wahabis. Bolshevist propaganda, the fatal danger. Mustapha Kemal. Inevitable return of anarchy. Losses to trade and the taxpayer. Basrah alone, no value. Hopeless weakness of present system. Must create a 'middle class', under British Protectorate. Small land-holdings, direct from Government. Possible development of immense resources, by scientific cultivation. Canals and irrigation. The only way!

AS TO OUR FUTURE policy in Mesopotamia, there are only two suggestions that have been put forward with sufficient vigour to merit serious examination.

The first is that we should completely evacuate the country and leave it to its fate. The second, that we should withdraw to the port of Basrah, holding under our control that city and its environs.

If we evacuate Mesopotamia, it would be interesting to attempt a forecast of what seems most likely to occur. Of the possibilities that I propose to portray, some are at least most probable. In the ever-changing kaleidoscope of Middle East intrigue, no man dare say more.

THE INS AND OUTS OF MESOPOTAMIA

I have indicated, at every point, this people's natural distaste for law and order, the patent profits of anarchy to their chiefs, and the manifold occasions for internal dissension which racial and religious prejudices are always at hand to inflame.

In this connection, I should perhaps explain more precisely why one of the terms exacted from us by Hussein of Mecca was a guarantee that his neighbour Ibn Saud should keep the peace, by which we are, in fact, involved in a generous subsidy paid monthly.

This Ibn Saud today represents the ruling dynasty of the sect of the Wahabis, whose headquarters at Riadh are, inconveniently for the faithful, comparatively close to Mecca. This proselytising sect was founded about 1720, by Muhammed ibn Abd al Wahab, in reaction against prevalent departures – in faith and practice – from the Word of the Quran and the Traditions of the Companion of the Prophet. It is, in short, a Unitarian Puritanism of the most rigid type. The founder met with the usual persecutions, and sought the aid of an important Sheikh – Muhammed ibn Saud, who, becoming a convert, proved an immense power. The tenets of the Wahabi declare that everything which was not done by the Prophet, or was not the custom in his days, is sin. All unnecessary adjuncts to worship, such as rosaries and charms, are peculiarly offensive. The wearing of silk clothes is forbidden. Smoking excites their fury above everything, while the last abomination is the giving of divine honour to saints by way of – among other means – pilgrimage to their shrines.

THE FUTURE

In his *Central and Eastern Arabia*, Palgrave mentions an amusing experience.

> 'Abd al Karim said: "The first of the great sins is the giving of divine honours to a creature." "Of course," I replied, "the enormity of such a sin is beyond all doubt. But if this be the first, there must be a second; what is it?" "Drinking the shameful (that is, smoking tobacco)," was the unhesitating answer. "And murder, adultery, and false witness!" I suggested. "God is merciful and forgiving," rejoined my friend; "that is, these are merely little sins." '

Such rigid formalism, of course, involved the enmity of both the Orthodox Sunni and the heretical Shia'. For it overthrew the authority of the four Orthodox Imams,[1] and declared that the shrines and the honour paid to the saints were the worst possible blasphemy.

They have twice sacked Medina and Mecca, plundering the Shrine of the Prophet and distributing its treasures among their troops. They have more than once turned their attention to the holy cities of Mesopotamia, sacking Kerbela itself, and only repulsed from Najaf by the surrounding wall, hastily erected against them.

Inevitably the feud against the house of the Shariff is kept alive by memories of days when Mecca was in their hands, and purged of idolatry. Mesopotamia presents an ever-present temptation

---

[1] These were the four great legalists who drew up the Sunnat, or Laws and Traditions of Islam. They must not be confounded with the Shia' Imams, for whom some miraculous Spirit of God is claimed by those who accept the doctrine of the Imamate.

before their eyes. It is already besprinkled with members of a secretly proselytising Akhwan, or brotherhood, which has spread over all parts of the Muslim world.

If they disturbed the peace under Turkish regime, they would inevitably overrun the country, once we withdrew our support from the eldest son of their hated neighbour and hereditary enemy whom we have placed over it.

They are, as I have already noted, even more bitter against the Shia' than the Sunni. Those who spared not Mecca or the Shrine of the Prophet himself at Medina, would give short shift to the shrines of the Imams at Najaf, Kerbela, Kadhimain, and Samarra, the very centre of the doctrines which, above all others, they are determined to destroy. An immediate and unprecedented conflagration, to which no man could set a sure limit, would inevitably arise throughout Persia, the Shia' stronghold, already impregnated, as it is, with Bolshevist propaganda.

It is extremely significant to remember that the partial withdrawal of British control in Mesopotamia in 1921, was coincident with a remarkable outbreak of Wahabi activity; and when certain Shamiyah leaders fled, after the revolution, they went to Riadh, and were, by their own account, most kindly received! Sir Percy Cox had the greatest difficulty in restraining Feisal from taking action against the Wahabis, for what he was pleased to regard as an incursion into his 'dominion'.

Persia is always more or less in a state of anarchy. Its utterly corrupt Government, the gross tyranny exercised by those in authority over the poverty-stricken peasant, and the extortions to which he is subject from a host of officials, whose pay is always months in arrears, the execrable appointments to important official positions, all render the country a perfect breeding-ground for the Bolshevist bacillus.

This is the gravest of all the problems of the East, to which the present success of Mustapha Kemal (I write in September 1922) adds ominous significance. The ever-restless Kurdish tribes, always used by the Turks for their dirtier work, would be only too pleased to join forces in an orgy of reckless massacre; and it is well known (if not to the general public) that no small proportion of the Red Army of Bolshevik Russia is Muslim. On the publication of the terms of peace with Turkey, Mustapha Kemal joined the Bolshevist headquarters in Asia Minor, whence he has lately emerged at the head of an all-conquering force, composed of what? It is assumed that *all* his troops are Turks; but we are now told that the rout of the Greeks was due to a large proportion of their army turning Bolshevist, and deserting, with shouts of 'Long live Lenin and Trotsky!'

Whether or not this be mere rumour, it is a fact that, on the fall of Smyrna, Mustapha Kemal officially thanked the Russian Soviet for their assistance, while we learn of an alliance between the Soviet and the Angora Government, who are ready to attack Roumania at a word from Mustapha Kemal. At present Mustapha Kemal is merely a Turkish General, but, though he is naturally regarded as something of a hero by Muslims, he in no sense officially represents Islam. It is, however, extraordinarily significant that he has declared his determination to appoint a *new Sultan*, and, were the power in his hands, it is surely obvious that he would select some whole-hearted supporter of his late allies. *Can we, or indeed can Europe, face an offensive and defensive alliance between Bolshevism and the Khaliph of all Islam?* I would here emphasise that the Bolshevist movement is *not* moribund, and that, once firmly established in the Middle East, for many years its endeavour, it would have secured an anchorage from which it would be almost impracticable to dislodge it.

It is not even necessary to state who would suffer most. If it be urged that European Powers would not permit our downfall, let it be remembered that the British Empire is a permanent source of jealousy to those same Powers and, could such a catastrophe be brought about without disturbing Europe, there is not one who would raise a finger in our defence. It is an ill wind that blows nobody any good, and it may yet prove that the present state of European credits and currency will open their eyes to their dependence upon our prosperity and show them that, if we fall – we shall not fall alone. But the final decision will not rest with the few wise men of each nation, but must be taken by the ordinary man in the street, who has no time for the study of such problems, and is content to form his opinions from the headlines of his daily paper. One is sometimes tempted to think that the special job of Lucifer, Star of the Morning (or the Morning Star), is that of Patron Saint of some sections of the world's Press!

THE FUTURE

A complete evacuation of Mesopotamia would almost certainly mean an invasion of the Wahabis, involving a general uprising throughout Persia. Mesopotamia, rent by religious strife and internecine feuds, would become the prey to murder, robbery, and general anarchy, *obviously ripe for the formation of a powerful Bolshevist confederacy between Islam and the Soviet*.

I do not enter into the question of the Armenian and other Christian minorities; but no conceivable guarantees in the world would ensure their safety, and it is hardly possible to doubt what the European conscience would have to say.

Other effects on the social life of the people as a whole would clearly follow, with consequences one could only estimate with dismay. All modern civilisation and progress would be wiped out. Trade with the Middle East and Persia would cease abruptly, and the inevitable torpid bankruptcy would add yet another burden to the credit system of the world, by which we all exist.

Sentimentalists, no doubt, scorn commercial considerations, but they will always influence the common-sense point of view. Mesopotamia has already absorbed a vast outpouring of British capital, of which an enormous amount has been spent on permanent improvements. To quote one instance: the development of the port at Basrah represents many millions of pounds. Our withdrawal would almost certainly involve the closing down of the port. Basrah now imports far more than it exports, and a very large proportion of the revenue of the country is derived from customs duties. But what country or firm would export to a land seething with internal strife and Bolshevism? Where would be the necessary security? What insurance company would underwrite propositions of such a nature? The late Captain Mann, a Political Officer, writing to the *Nation*, says:

'During the war there was here an interregnum after the Turks withdrew and before our occupation became effective. What happened? On the stretch of twenty miles of river where I live, no less than seven different tribes took a toll from every boat that went up or down the river, as it entered the territory of each. This is quite bluntly what cultural "autonomy" means to the Arab, namely, the right to strip the foreigner; and the foreigner is the man in the next tribe.'

Without its customs duties, the country would go bankrupt, the port fall to ruins, and the already invested capital be irretrievably lost. The same line of reasoning is applicable to railways, buildings, and irrigation.

The Empire and the governance of the world is, from one aspect, a business concern. Can a politician be justified in putting any other consideration before this? If business and sentiment can be combined, it is all to the good.

On these grounds, then, a complete evacuation seems to be impossible. We have an alternative policy associated with the name of Mr. Asquith – a partial evacuation, i.e. a withdrawal from Baghdad, holding under our control only Basrah and its environs. It is extraordinarily difficult to see what would be gained. It is true that there would be an immediate reduction in expenditure, but at what

THE FUTURE

cost? The position and the power of the Jewish community has been ignored, or forgotten. As in every country, they are the progressives, the heads of the big business houses, who control the greater proportion of the capital of the country. They live almost entirely in Baghdad. Were such a scheme seriously contemplated, there would be a complete withdrawal of all business from Baghdad, a drying-up of all the local financial springs, a large emigration from the city, and the bankrupt capital of a bankrupt country, seething with rebellion, at the very gates of Basrah City.

We should have no control over other portions of the country, in which must be produced a similar condition of insecurity to that which complete withdrawal would, admittedly, involve. Should we gain anything which could be described as even a remote return for all the British money invested in the country? The occupation of Basrah would not be a cheap activity, while the upkeep of the port would add another burden to the tax-payer, without any hope of an eventual return.

It seems therefore that either a complete evacuation or partial withdrawal from Mesopotamia is unthinkable from the business point of view. From the standpoint of politics it would spell ruin to the country, a ruin which, in its aftermath, would have an incalculable effect on the British Empire in the East, and on the world at large. Mesopotamia – though it stinks in the nostrils of the British tax-payer – is none the less in many respects like unto Achilles' heel. By geographical position, it is the heart of the Islamic peoples; its past history is one of rebellion, anarchy, and nihilism. Were it left to itself, there can be little doubt that it would become a Middle-East Bolshevist Power, the nucleus and focus of all the evil forces in the world.

At the same time, the present inanity, which passes for government in the country, seems futile, extravagant, and utterly unbusinesslike. Beyond the fact that our mere presence in Mesopotamia exerts a tremendous moral influence, as a sedative on the forces of disorder, it serves no useful purpose. The force at our disposal, while ample to preserve internal order, would be powerless against an organised force from the north, such as might well be undertaken by Kemal, drunk with victory, in conjunction with the Kurdish tribes. Neither is it strong enough to control anything more than local risings. Its upkeep is not cheap. One year of the Feisal regime has shown a large *decrease* in revenue, with an *increase* in corruption and inefficiency. It has fostered discontent and intrigue among the tribes, sick of the insolent dishonesty of the Baghdadi Effendi and his confrères. The municipalities of Basrah and Baghdad find it increasingly difficult to pay their way. Trade is stagnant, and merchants are in a parlous condition. Such has been the result of the present administration *in one year*.

How, then, can we make a paying concern out of a country which the war has thrust into our hands, from which it is impossible to withdraw and in which millions of British capital have been invested?

Certainly not by self-government, and certainly not by the half-and-half, effete, and crippled ad-

THE FUTURE

ministration in existence at the present moment. If Mesopotamia is to be made a paying concern – and that it can be so made I am convinced – it will only be done by development of all its resources, and by internal security that would attract trade. This means an absolutely firm Government, backed by sufficient forces to quell any disturbance that might arise. After all, even in the most enlightened states of Europe, it is force that keeps us in the van of civilisation and, whatever may be the verdict of idealistic sentimentalists, proves the final arbiter.

I would wish to make it quite clear that I do not advocate a rigid Prussianism, a crushing of the Arab people, an 'exploitation' of the simple peasant. I believe that it is possible to produce a self-governing Mesopotamia (in the *real* sense) in, say, one hundred years' time; but I am also convinced that it is hardly likely to be done in less, and will never be accomplished under the present regime.

To secure an equitable return for invested capital within a reasonable time, and to train the people in the art of government, I believe we must make Mesopotamia a British Protectorate. It should so remain, until its peoples have learned sufficient discipline to be assured of some equilibrium and permanent progress. In an undertaking of this size, a quick return cannot be looked for. The one unanswerable criticism of the present policy is that it renders any return for money invested an impossibility. It involves an annual outgoing from the tax-payer, with no possible prospect of any incoming.

THE INS AND OUTS OF MESOPOTAMIA

To put the country permanently on its legs all pan-Arab sentimentalists must go. They will have plenty of scope in about seventy years' time, but they have come on the stage much too early. How, then, should we proceed?

We must first realise the almost complete absence of a middle class, except, of course, in the towns. As the enormous majority of the population is tribal, these are, after all, of little account. The gulf between the Sheikhs and their 'fellaliyeh' (peasants), between the Religious Hierarchy and the common folk, is unbridgeable. All intrigue and rebellion against authority is invariably incited by the Ruasa (or leaders), to serve their own ends. We can check the power of these robber-barons, along either of two lines. By the creation of a middle class from the superior 'fellaliyeh' or inferior Sheikh – represented today by a few fairly well-to-do Sirakil (the lesser chiefs) – or by a grant of small holdings to the 'fellaliyeh', who would then pay revenue direct to the Government, instead of to the Sheikh. The latter method would probably be the more efficient. It would eventually have the effect of producing just that class that would undermine the pernicious influence of the Sheikh, at present largely responsible for tribal discontent through his extortions.

As an example of what frequently occurs, an infuriated tribesman burst into my office one day and told me that I had ruined him! On inquiry, it was found that the plot of land which he tilled would, in a normal year, produce about one ton of rice, the price of which would be about 250 rupees. He, like all the 'fellaliyeh', could neither read nor

THE FUTURE

write; and his Sheikh claimed nearly all his rice, on the pretence of a revenue demand for about 200 rupees. Now the 'fellah' knew perfectly well that Government did not require more than a third of his crop, while another third was due to the Sheikh as rent. He naturally protested; only to have waved before him a mysterious piece of paper, on which he saw some marks supposed to be Government orders. He was, in fact, actually on his way to sell some of his rice and household goods, when fury gave him sufficient courage to come and see me personally. The matter was, of course, rectified, but had he not done so, the Sheikh would simply have stolen from him about 60 rupees for his own pocket!

Such a system of small holdings would present less difficulty than might at first appear. The Tapu Department, to which reference has already been made, is busy mapping and surveying the whole country. The work is nearly complete, and will disclose the *real* holdings of Sheikh and Sirkal, thus removing the insecure tenure which has been a permanent source of discontent and violence. The illiterate and ignorant 'fellah' has been powerless against the semi-educated cunning and wealth of the Sheikh or Syed, neither of whom will stop at forgery, or the compulsory signing of deeds, to make good his claims to any land he may covet. He invariably tells the 'fellah' that he is acting under orders from the Government and can thus easily foster discontent whenever the time seems ripe for rebellion.

I can think of no other means which would so quickly produce a peaceful settlement of the country. The land would be more efficiently and more economically worked. Our personal dealing with the 'fellah' would involve a greater control over the methods of cultivation, effecting, among other benefits, an immense saving of water, which would enable additional tracts of land to be put under cultivation. The resources of the country are really enormous, if they were properly developed. The Arab methods of irrigation are so hopelessly extravagant that there is not now sufficient water to put fresh areas under cultivation. One example will show this. The rice cultivator of Southern India employs about 1½ cusecs of water to each acre. The Shamiyah Sheikhs employ about 20 cusecs! It is true that they produce a larger crop per acre, but their methods are purely temporary, and will soon cause the whole land under cultivation to be water-logged and salted up. Thousands of acres of cultivable land have been already put out of cultivation. They have no idea of scientific drainage, and tens of thousands of acres have been reduced to vast swamps. There is no manner of doubt that these can be redeemed, but such work would be impossible under any Government that depends on Islamic influence for its progressive policy.

As an example of what might be done, there was a canal in the Hillah area which had been useless for years. It was completed in 1918, directly we had a strong enough force to compel the tribesman to do a certain amount of manual labour for his own benefit. The following season no less than 30,000 acres yielded their harvest of wheat and barley – and this from land which had lain fallow

THE FUTURE

for so long, that no living man could remember when it had last produced a crop! This enormous acreage of new cultivation naturally attracted the tribes, who had formerly existed by robbery and the looting of their more peaceful neighbours. An area of country famous for its crime then settled down to days of peace.

One or two other examples of what is possible may be of interest. In the area of Fellujah, an ancient canal known as 'the Saqlawiyah' was once again put into working order. This brought the surrounding land into cultivation again, the area being no less than 250,000 acres of remarkably rich soil, of which 40,000 is perennial. The Political Officer who was in charge of the work, writes very significantly:

'Political pressure was throughout necessary to keep the tribal labour supplied up to full numbers. At the conclusion of the work, however, enthusiasm increased and labour worked well to open up the canal. *Irrigation in this district is now sufficient to supply every Arab with cultivation . . . In various instances, owners of other property are now unable to cultivate the whole of it, for lack of fellaliyeh, who naturally prefer to cultivate their own land if they can get any.* In short, the area of irrigated land is now fully sufficient for the whole population of this district.'

I suppose there still *are* people who would call this 'exploiting' the Arab!

The point that I desire to enforce is that, with a strong Government, the country can be made a paying concern. These examples might be multiplied over and over again. Reports were coming in from all over the country to the same effect, during *a temporary* administration established in war! It is not difficult to imagine the possibilities of the country, under a similar permanent Government. It would be of the greatest interest to know just what, if anything, has been done under Feisal and his administration. It is most likely that canals have been allowed to silt up, and large areas once more left in unproductive idleness.

But apart from ground crops, vast developments are possible in fruit growing. In the Shamiyah area alone, the value of the date-crop of 1919 approximated to 274,000,000 rupees;[1] and that is nothing compared to the date-gardens around Basrah. Baqubah is a vast fruit-growing area, specialising particularly in oranges, which could be enormously developed under a Government sufficiently strong to supervise proper and scientific methods of cultivation. Besides dates and oranges, the country grows peaches, apricots, lemons, limes, sweet limes, figs, grapes, pomegranates, melons, and water-melons in profusion. In the production of vegetables it is singularly rich. These include carrots, radishes, pumpkins, beetroot, tomatoes, cucumbers, French beans, baqalizh, turnips, onions, and many other varieties. At present these are all produced without any kind of scientific knowledge, and only in such quantities as the Arab requires for bare subsistence.

It is difficult, in fact, to assign a limit to the value of its products, were the country developed

---

[1] In this year the market rate was about double that of a normal year.

THE FUTURE

to its utmost capacity. But one thing is certain, that such development, combined with the increase of trade which the resulting peace and security would bring about, could not only amply support its own administration, but would more than repay past and future investors.

On the other hand, there can be no doubt that an efficient administration cannot be set up from any ex-employees of the Syrian, or the Meccan, Court. It will need British Officers, who have been trained to the art of government, and who, if they seem severe to the undisciplined Arab, are at any rate thoroughly trusted by their subjects.

At present, the tax-payer is asked to subscribe about six million pounds per annum to keep Feisal on the throne. He will never see any return, and it is but poor comfort for him to realise that the great majority of the inhabitants of Mesopotamia is as heartily sick of the present state of affairs as he is himself. An efficient administration, manned by experienced British Officers with local subordinates, might certainly cost more at first; but, on the other hand, such an investment would inevitably produce development sufficient to repay the investor again and again.

Let us not hear any more about Arab 'aspirations', 'cultural autonomy', and such like sentimentalities. They have already done an infinite amount of harm, and may do irretrievable damage. I believe the Arab *will* learn, in the course of long years, the advantages of self-discipline and co-operation, but at present he is nowhere near the beginning of the alphabet. He has fine qualities, rarely in evidence, which occasionally reveal what

THE INS AND OUTS OF MESOPOTAMIA

he may attain. But until their manifestation becomes a normal state of affairs, it is grossly unfair to bolster him up with ideas of his own importance and greatness. I cannot conclude better than in the words used by the late Captain Mann in his letter to the *Nation*, from which I have quoted before:

'I believe that we can build up an Arab Government; I think it is a task profoundly worth attempting; but I am sure that you must give us time. We shall pay for it by being occasionally murdered; and you at home will have to endure taunts of Imperialism, perfidy, and the like. If you insist on turning us out, you will let loose incalculable forces of destruction.'

APPENDIX

THE ANGLO-FRENCH DECLARATION

(Copy of the translation published in the *Morning Post*, 8th November 1918.)

The object aimed at by France and Great Britain in prosecuting in the East the war let loose by the ambition of Germany is the complete and definitive emancipation of the peoples so long oppressed by the Turks, and the establishment of Governments and national administrations deriving their authority from the initiative and free choice of the indigenous populations.

In order to carry out these intentions France and Great Britain are at one in encouraging and assisting the establishment of indigenous Governments and administrations in Syria and Mesopotamia, now liberated by the Allies, and in the territories the liberation of which they are engaged in securing, and in recognising these as soon as they are actually established. Far from wishing to impose on the populations of these regions any particular institutions, they are only concerned to ensure by their support and by adequate assistance the regular working of Governments and administrations freely chosen by themselves. To secure impartial and equal justice for all, to facilitate the economic development of the country by inspiring and encouraging local initiative, to favour the diffusion of education, to put an end to dissensions that have

THE INS AND OUTS OF MESOPOTAMIA

been too long taken advantage of by Turkish policy, such is the policy which the two Allied Governments uphold in the liberated territories.

www.ingramcontent.com/pod-product-compliance
Lightning Source LLC
Chambersburg PA
CBHW060151050426
42446CB00013B/2774